Best CX Ever For Providers

150+ pages of tips, strategies, tactics, examples, advice, and best practices.

Best CX Ever For Providers

How To Provide
The Best Customer Experiences
Every Time

Kirstla Ostler & Shawn Ostler

www.bestcxever.com

Copyright © 2024 Best CX Ever LLC

All rights reserved.

No portion of this book may be reproduced in any form without written permission from the publisher or author except as permitted by U.S. copyright law.

This publication is designed to provide accurate and authoritative information in regard to the subject matter covered. It is sold with the understanding that neither the author nor the publisher is engaged in rendering legal, investment, accounting, or other professional services. While the publisher and author have used their best efforts in preparing this book, they make no representations or warranties with respect to the accuracy or completeness of the contents of this book and specifically disclaim any implied warranties of merchantability or fitness for a particular purpose. No warranty may be created or extended by sales representatives or written sales materials. The advice and strategies contained herein may not be suitable for your situation. You should consult with a professional when appropriate. Neither the publisher nor the author shall be liable for any loss of profit or any other commercial damages, including but not limited to special, incidental, consequential, personal, or other damages.

Kirstla,

Thank you for your talent, skills, and hard work. They are the reasons we have this book and have helped so many providers. I am very proud to have my name on this book right next to yours.

Shawn

Acknowledgements

We want to thank all the providers who have shared their thoughts, experiences, and advice with us. We are grateful for everything we learned together, and we are sorry if we left anyone out.

Hillary, Spencer, Nancy, Linda, Ryan, Jennifer, Kayley, Amanda, Scott, Mathew, Megan, Rich, Karrell, David, Jessica, Phil, Adam, Michael, Jake, Samantha, Johnathan, Leslie, Michelle, TJ, Willy, Louie, Marty, Deda, Rene, Christie, Lila, Jessica, Lisa, Lilly, Shannon, Taylor, Todd, Raja, and Chrissy.

Table Of Contents

Who This Book Is For 1
Where The Best Practices Came From 3
Who Are We? 7
The Customer Experience 11
Customer Service Roles 15
How To Provide The Best Experiences 17
Best Practices 23
Preparing To Provide Service 27
    Be Prepared 29
    Develop And Maintain Core Skills 35
    Record And Resolve Issues 41
    Record And Reply To Feedback 47
    Practice, Practice, Practice 53
Providing Service 59
    Always Use "How To" 61
    Answer Confidently 69
    Write Everything Down 77
    Be Polite 85
    Communicate Clearly 95
    Listen To Understand 105
    Be A Guide 113
    Same Way Every Time 121
    The Power Of "Oh..." 129
    Don't Judge 135
    Avoid Negativity 145
    Reset Button 153
    Use Recovery Time 161
Improving Service 167
    Bitch Sessions 169
    Power-Up Sessions 175
    Continuous Improvement 181
Summary 187
How We Can Help You 191
Appendix 193
Bibliography 199
Author Bios 203

Who This Book Is For

We wrote this book for everyone who interacts with customers and provides customer service, whether it's through phone calls, emails, face-to-face interactions, chats, video calls, social media, etc.

We have learned a lot about what it takes to provide outstanding customer experiences over the years and want to share what we have learned. The best practices, tips, and advice in this book were developed over the last 25 years with the following goals in mind:

- Learn to provide the same service for every customer, no matter how I feel or how rude the last customer was.
- Max out my monthly bonus and get a yearly pay raise.
- Achieve desired promotions.
- Improve my customer satisfaction ratings.
- Raise my level of job satisfaction.
- Increase conversion rates and commissions.
- Generate more referrals.
- Achieve higher quality and compliance scores.
- Deal with the negativity of customer service and let it go at the end of the day.

We can provide each customer with the best experience every time we interact with them, even when things do not go well. This book will teach you exactly how we provide our customers with the best experiences possible every single time.

Where The Best Practices Came From

We had both been working in customer service for about six years. At that time, Kirstla worked for a shipping company, and I worked for a credit card company. One day, I mentioned that a team leader told me I was one of the best reps and asked me to share some advice and tips with their team. I tried but struggled and could not figure out what to tell them.

I ended up sharing the same generic tips I got during training, and I felt terrible because I wanted to do more. Kirstla said the same thing happened to her, and she also could not figure out how to explain it. We built up our skills and knowledge by interacting with customers for years. It seemed natural to us that it was hard to put into words.

We continued talking about it and wondered how we could share our knowledge. Kirstla had just been promoted to trainer, and I was applying to be a team leader. While talking, we realized it would benefit both of us if we could develop a way to share our experience with other representatives and teach them what we know.

We realized there needed to be actual definitions for the skills and techniques we used every day. After many long conversations, we realized we could create and use those definitions to teach others.

Over the next few years, we analyzed ourselves and our interactions. We started documenting the successful tactics and techniques and recording any patterns we recognized. We also began studying other providers and defining their techniques and strategies. Throughout this research, we learned about the concept of a "best practice." We used the tactics, techniques, and patterns to build a list of best practices.

Each best practice had a definition and instructions for implementing the practice during any interaction. We started using these best practices to teach our trainees and team members our knowledge and skills. The people we taught began to rise to the top and quickly.

We both changed employers and worked in completely different industries during this time. We took the best practices with us and taught them to our new trainees and team members, and our teams quickly rose to the top. We realized these practices could and should be applied in every industry.

We started researching and analyzing other providers in these new industries and many others. We found more providers using these same techniques and began working as consultants with many of the companies we studied.

This led us to understand that every industry should use these practices. We started a training and consulting business and taught our clients these practices. We continue to analyze ourselves, our clients, and many other companies and regularly refine and expand our list of best practices.

This book is the culmination of our experience, research, and development. It includes all the best practices that must be applied to provide the best experiences possible every time. It includes advice, tips, and tricks from skilled and experienced providers in many industries.

Who Are We?

We are customer service providers, just like you, and we want to share what we have learned during our years of service. Each of us has worked in customer service for over 25 years. We have worked for major shipping companies, credit card companies, retail stores, cell phone providers, pharmacies, hotels, and market research firms. We have also worked for real estate brokers, property management companies, small restaurants, small shops, catering companies, and food trucks.

We were always among the top performers. We quickly rose to the top when we started new jobs at different companies. Our coaches and managers were always impressed with us and how well we worked with customers, especially when they were upset.

We have been promoted and worked in different positions. We have been advisors/gurus, QA, trainers, coaches, and managers. Some of us own other businesses and employ customer service providers like you.

We know who you are and what you go through daily as providers because we also went through it. We wanted our day-to-day work experience to improve, so we set some goals and made some changes.

These are the exact goals that we set for ourselves:

- We both want to provide the same level of service to every customer, no matter how we feel or how rude the last customer was.
- We want to max out our monthly bonuses and get a yearly pay raise.
- Shawn wants to be a team leader, and Kirstla wants to be a trainer.
- We want to improve our customer satisfaction ratings and keep them high every month.
- We want to like our jobs again.
- Shawn wants more conversions to get a higher commission.
- Kirstla wants to lower her average handle time.
- We want more referrals from our customers.
- We want to achieve the highest quality and performance scores possible.
- We want to deal with the negativity that comes with doing customer service and let it go at the end of the day.

Over time, we developed the best practices you will learn. We implemented these practices in our jobs every day and saw instant results. The best practices helped us achieve every one of the goals listed above, and they will work for you, too.

We love what we do. We are lifelong service providers and always strive to be the best we can be. We believe every customer deserves the best experience when interacting with us. As providers, we are capable of providing the best experience every time.

We are excited to share our knowledge and experience. We are happy you have chosen to learn from us and thrilled it will take you less time to become the best!

The Customer Experience

Most customers want a simple shopping experience where they can have their questions answered and problems solved by someone kind, professional, and happy to help. When they need help or have an issue, they want it fixed quickly and with as little effort as possible.

The customer's experience will determine whether they continue their business with you or go elsewhere. A great experience will entice a customer to return, and they will share what happened with their friends and family.

As a provider, you have control over this experience. You can make any experience fantastic, and we will teach you how.

You need to understand the difference between customer service and the customer's experience.

Here is the definition of "experience":

- *An event or occurrence that leaves an impression on someone*
  Encyclopedia.com

- *The way that something happens and how it makes you feel*
  Cambridge Dictionary

The definition of "service" is:

- *The act of dealing with customers in a store, restaurant, or hotel by taking their orders, showing or selling them goods, etc.*
  Cambridge Dictionary

- *Being of help, use or benefit*
  Merriam-Webster

The customer's experience is their thoughts, feelings, and perceptions of their interaction with you, both during and after. Service is helping the customer complete a task or process, like completing their purchase or solving an issue. An interaction without service will always result in a bad experience, but there needs to be more than just service to provide a great experience. You must be of service and leave the customer with a good impression and memorable feelings.

Each interaction you have with the customer is an opportunity to influence their feelings and impressions of you and the company you work for.

The experience you provide can be simple and free. It does not require giving customers a discount or something for free. The best customer experiences are memorable and entice them to be a repeat customer.

Why It's Important

A great experience will develop trust between you and the customer. If a customer is comfortable interacting with you, they will return repeatedly. They will make larger purchases and are more likely to pay for upgrades or premium services. If you work on commission or bonus, you will earn higher payouts.

Repeat customers provide job security. If you provide great experiences, you can feel secure in your job and start growing your career. You will be able to work for any company and will be considered for promotions and raises.

Repeat customers also provide referrals; they will tell their friends and family about you and your company. Word of mouth is free and is the most effective form of marketing. Every good experience you provide is a chance to get a referral.

More Companies Are Prioritizing The Customer Experience (CX)

Recently, many companies have created new jobs, from entry-level positions to the executive level, focusing entirely on the customer experience. This is because they have realized how important each customer's experience is.

- Customer Experience Rep - CropX
- Customer Success Associate - CINQ Partnership
- Customer Care Manager - MasteryPrep
- Customer Experience Strategist - Department of the Treasury
- Customer Experience Mobile Expert - T-Mobile
- Radiology Scheduler CX - SquarePeg
- Customer Experience Quality Assessor - PharmaCentra, LLC
- Customer Experience Specialist - Ascen
- Customer Success Specialist - Ora
- Client Success Associate - INFUSE

The appendix at the back of this book provides more details about these jobs and many more available ones.

As an expert in providing great experiences, you will have access to these jobs and can go as high up the ladder as you want.

The advice, examples, and tips in this book have been used for years by providers in every industry to provide the best experiences for their customers. If you implement these best practices, you will start providing the best experiences while interacting with your customers.

Customer Service Roles

Providing customer service requires many different jobs and responsibilities. These jobs are also known by many names: agent, representative, associate, cashier, barista, manager, coach, interaction specialist, etc.

During our research, we found every job title fell into one of three classifications: those who interact with customers, those who lead a team of providers, and those who can change policies or procedures.

A provider is anyone who interacts with prospects and customers at any time. They are the front line and have direct contact with customers. This includes anyone who communicates and interacts with customers and prospects, everyone in the organization, and all departments from top to bottom.

A coach is anyone who leads a team of providers. They are the first person a provider will approach for help. They are responsible for their providers' skill development, performance, and quality scores. They are among the most important people to a provider.

An owner is a decision-maker who defines the rules and policies related to customer service.

We are all responsible for creating the best experiences possible and must work together. As providers, we have the largest opportunity to affect the outcome of each interaction. This book is for providers and contains everything you need to create the best experiences.

How To Provide The Best Experiences

It is a journey from point A, where you are now, to point B, where you provide the best experience possible during every interaction. You must continuously grow your customer service knowledge and skills throughout the journey.

This book contains tips, examples, strategies, and best practices from successful, experienced providers across different industries. It was compiled over the last 25+ years as we worked to become the best providers possible.

Your journey does not have to take that long. You can jump-start it by learning from providers who already have experience. Most of our trainees complete the journey within two years.

We have learned that incrementally improving your skills is the best strategy for getting from point A to point B. Trying to make significant or many improvements simultaneously is overwhelming, and you will make little progress.

> *Small disciplines repeated with consistency every day lead to great achievements gained slowly over time.*
>
> John C. Maxwell

You need a process to follow, one you will repeat regularly. This is called an iterative process. In each iteration, you will make minor improvements that build upon each other until you reach your goal, point B.

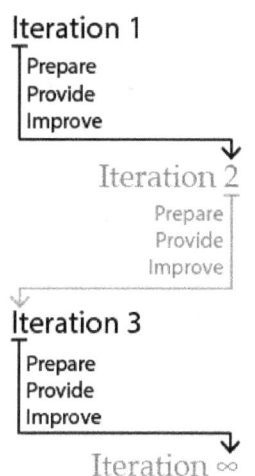

Over time, we have developed a simple and effective process. It has three distinct phases: prepare, provide, and improve.

During the first phase, you will spend time learning and practicing to prepare yourself to provide the best experiences possible.

During the provide phase, you will interact with customers and put your new skills to work.

During the last phase, improve, you will look for areas to improve and create actionable recommendations for yourself.

With these recommendations, you will start a new iteration and implement them in the prepare phase. When you feel prepared, you will move to the provide phase and put your new skills to work.

Some improvements will require more time and effort than others. This process is designed to be flexible. Each phase can last as long as you need, or the phases can be completed in a short amount of time. You can also complete multiple iterations on the same day.

It will take time to gain all the needed experience, but you won't have to wait to reap the rewards. Each practice has examples, tips, strategies, etc., that you can apply immediately.

To fully understand the best practices, you must try them with real customers and then analyze the outcome. With each customer interaction, you will gain more experience and a deeper understanding of the practices and their benefits. The more you interact with customers, the faster you will grow.

The Prepare Phase

Success depends upon previous preparation, and without such preparation, there is sure to be failure.

Confucious

During this phase, implement any recommendations you have and take time to practice, preparing yourself to provide the best experiences possible. By the end of this phase, you should feel prepared to interact with customers if you don't stay in this phase and keep practicing. Do what it takes to feel prepared before you start interacting with customers.

Review policies and procedures to refresh your memory and look for updates. If anything has changed, take the time to learn the changes, ask questions, and practice until you are comfortable with them.

Learn from other providers and practice with them. Act out real-life scenarios and actual interactions you will have with your customers. The more accurate your scenarios are, the more prepared you will feel when they actually happen.

You should spend about 5-20% of your time in this phase.

The Provide Phase

All good thoughts and ideas mean nothing without action.

Mahatma Gandhi

A plan without action is not a plan. It's a speech.

T. Boone Pickens

This is your time to shine! You will spend most of your time in this phase, about 60-90%. When you interact with customers, try to provide the best experience possible. Keep this book available and use it as a quick reference.

If you have made improvement plans, follow them as best you can. The best time to implement any new changes is while working with customers. You will deal with real scenarios and customer issues and have to think on your feet.

Keep a list of difficult or complex tasks, awkward moments or conversations, and any questions you have during your interactions.

During this phase, you will receive feedback from customers, your team leader, QA, etc. Add this feedback to your list of things you can improve. Feedback can be hard to accept, but having other people's perspectives on your performance is very important. Anyone who provides you feedback has already put in the effort required to find something you can improve. This will save you a lot of time and work.

The Improve Phase

Change alone doesn't bring growth but you cannot have growth without change.

John C. Maxwell

During this phase, you will look for possible improvements. You should review your past interactions, observe other providers, and ask your team leader for suggestions. Create a list of the potential improvements you can implement.

If your list contains many possible improvements, you will implement one or two during the next cycle and the rest during the following cycles.

Create Actionable Recommendations

For each area you want to improve, create actionable recommendations for yourself. Define specific actions that will help you improve. Do not recommend something you will never be able to accomplish.

For example, if you want to increase your customer satisfaction rating (CSAT), you could recommend being nicer to customers, but this will go nowhere because it is not specific. A better recommendation would be always to say thank you when a customer answers your question.

Break big recommendations into smaller, easier-to-implement ones. You should make these changes incrementally. Work on smaller improvements until you have achieved your bigger goal.

For each recommendation, make a plan for implementing it. The plan can be very simple. For example, Create a sticky note that says "Ask Question? Say Thank You!" and put it on your screen. Having a plan will help during the provide phase when you get busy. You can read the plan over again and start working on it.

Once you have plans for your recommendations, it is time to start a new cycle. Move to the "Prepare" phase and implement your plans.

Best Practices

What is a best practice?

- *A procedure that has been shown by research and experience to produce optimal results and that is established or proposed as a standard suitable for widespread adoption.*

                                                                    Merriam-Webster

The best way to share our knowledge and experience is by defining the best practices we follow. We have tried to explain the practices in a way that is simple and easy to remember.

You can review the practices anytime, so it's like having us whispering in your ear to help guide you.

Each practice has a "Hard Definition," which explains its ideal implementation. However, a perfect implementation is optional. We provide many different examples of how to implement them. You can choose the most effective implementation for you and your industry.

Developing new habits will require dedication, and perfecting the practices will require hard work. If you put in the time and effort, they will change how you do your job and how you feel about it and will help you get a promotion or higher bonuses.

We have separated the best practices into three sections to help you: "Prepare to Provide Service", "Provide Service", and "Improve Service." The practices are not required to be used in this order. You will achieve the best results by combining multiple practices to provide the best experience possible.

Our goal was to make it as easy as possible to implement each practice so they can be implemented all at once or incrementally, which allows you to make these changes at a pace that works for you. If you decide to implement one practice at a time, you will still achieve all the benefits from that practice. We designed the practices this way to help make them easier to implement. Each best practice can be implemented for free without your employer's support.

Prepare To Provide

- Be Prepared
- Develop and Maintain Core Skills
- Record And Resolve Issues
- Record and Reply To Feedback
- Practice, Practice, Practice

Provide Service

- Always Use "How-To"
- Answer Confidently
- Write Everything Down
- Be Polite
- Communicate Clearly
- Listen To Understand
- Be A Guide
- Same Way Every Time
- The Power of "Oh..."
- Don't Judge
- Avoid Negativity
- Reset Button
- Use Recovery Time

Improve Service

- Bitch Sessions
- Power-Up Sessions
- Provider Your Unique Experience
- Continuous Improvement

Your Resource For Great Customer Experiences

We want you to use this book as your customer experience resource or workbook. It is your "Go-To" resource when you need help providing a great experience or improving your skills.

We want you to write it in, make notes, and highlight important areas. Take it with you everywhere you provide service. Write down your plans and strategies for implementing the practices so you always have them with you. When you need help, go to your notes.

Each best practice includes customer service stories from our interactions with customers and the providers we have worked with over the years that almost every provider can relate to.

We will define "What" each best practice is, "Why It's Important", and "How To" perform or implement the practice. Each practice also has a "Hard Definition," which is a perfect definition of the practice, but this is not the only way to implement the practice or the "required" way. You can implement the practice in any way, and you will still receive the benefits it provides.

We have left a few pages at the end of each practice for you to take notes and develop your strategies.

Preparing To Provide Service

In this section, we will teach you the best practices that you will use when preparing to provide service. Preparing to provide service means you must be ready before trying to provide service. Great service and excellent experiences start with being prepared.

The Best Practices Used to Prepare to Provide Service:

- Be Prepared
- Develop and Maintain Core Skills
- Record and Resolve Issues
- Record and Reply to Feedback
- Practice, Practice, Practice

Be Prepared

I felt behind and stressed the whole day.

While working as a representative in chat, I was operating on auto-pilot, and I forgot to open some of my systems at the beginning of the day. We had a queue, and I got two chats right after I signed in. I did not realize my systems were not open until I went to access their accounts. Now, I was trying to respond to two chats and open up several systems at the same time.

I was surprised at how stressed and anxious it made me feel. I usually can answer a customer's question in chat within a few minutes, but this time, it took me over 5 minutes, and both customers sent a message saying, "Are you still there?" I was so embarrassed and trying to hurry. It made me so anxious. I didn't like how this made me feel; it lasted all day. Now, I ensure I am a few minutes early to open my systems and feel ready all day instead of stressed.

"I'm sorry, I am just waiting for my system to load."

One of the credit card companies we worked for had a system that took at least 7 minutes to load, sometimes up to 15 minutes. We all knew how long it took, and it became an inside joke for us. If the system was not open and loaded before you took a call, you would have to stall while it loaded, which was always awkward, especially if it was a repeat customer who had had to wait before. They would get very frustrated and start to demand help now.

We would make up reasons why we were waiting:

- "I'm sorry, I need to restart my system."
- "Oh, I am sorry. My system is forcing me to sign in again."
- "That's weird; my system is still loading. I will try again."
- "It will take a bit to pull up that information. Can I put you on hold?"
- "I need to contact another department to get that information for you. Can you hold for a few minutes?"

There were many others we all used. Some customers were willing to wait, but many were upset and said, "I will call back later." We always got negative responses to the survey that popped up at the end of the call, which affected my monthly bonus.

"Sorry, I just need a moment."

I have terrible allergies, especially during spring and fall. I always try to have a water bottle with me. If I don't, my throat dries out, and I start coughing. Sometimes uncontrollably. If I have water, I can turn on my mute and take a drink, which helps me get through the call. I remember one time it was so bad that I had to walk away from my desk to get a drink while I was still on the call. Luckily, the customer was still there when I returned to my call.

"I think she is having a bad day."

One day, I came to work really upset. I had been having a rough day and was mad at the world. I avoided everyone I usually say hi to on the way in because I did not want to talk to anyone. When I took my first call, you could hear in my voice that I did not want to be there. I did not say anything rude to the customer, but I did not do anything to be friendly either. I did not say sorry, or please, or thank you. I could have been more friendly and happy. I begrudgingly answered their questions, and they could tell I was annoyed.

I explained to one customer that I could not do what they wanted me to do for them, but they just kept asking for it. After asking for the third time and hearing no, they asked to speak to my supervisor. When I transferred the call, I overheard the customer say to the supervisor, "I think she is having a bad day."

When I heard that, I instantly felt terrible that I was not friendly to the customer. I could still not do what they wanted, but I could have been polite, happy, and friendly in delivering the news. My first call of the day escalated because I was not ready to provide service.

What Is "Be Prepared"?

It is a simple but highly effective practice. It involves being ready in our physical environment and mental headspace to provide service before we start interacting with customers. We should ensure everything we need is ready so there are no awkward pauses, and we are not distracted while trying to help our customers. Take the time to prepare before your shift starts and after your breaks and meals.

Why It's Important

We want to provide the best experience possible during every interaction. We need to be ready before the interaction starts. If we are prepared before we start, we can use our skills and experience to help the customer and make a great first impression.

Your first interactions will set the tone for the rest of your day, making it one of the most important things you can do before providing service.

You must be prepared to handle any interaction to have the best day possible. Being unprepared makes you feel rushed and behind all day. You will get less work done, and then you will be behind.

When you are ready to handle the next interaction, you will have more confidence when working with customers and feel prepared for any situation, even the bad ones.

> **Hard Definition:**
>
> Be prepared physically, mentally, and emotionally to provide service before you start your first interaction.

How To "Be Prepared"

Exactly what you do to prepare will depend on where you work or your industry. In a remote work environment, you will have computer systems and applications to log in to. You may have the till for your register in a store or a radio, gloves, and a box cutter. Even though what we do to prepare may differ, the concept is still the same.

Keep a checklist of everything you need. As you work, update the checklist so you don't miss any steps. Whenever you have to sign into something, start the program, get permissions, etc. If you need something throughout the workday, add it to your checklist, and you will have it ready next time.

When I start a new job, I create bookmarks and shortcuts for every system I have to use, making them easier to find and open. I ensure I have water, cough drops, snacks, pens, paper, etc. I get there early so I can set things up before I get started. After a while, I noticed things were improving; I felt better, less anxious, and more prepared to do my job.

If you use a web browser for many programs, many will allow you to set up a profile or multiple profiles. When you select the profile, it will open all the saved pages. Create a profile for each department you work in or even for various clients.

Mentally Prepared

Being mentally prepared is just as important as being physically prepared and having all your computer systems up and running. The stresses of your personal life will affect your interactions.

- Kids, Babysitter, School, etc.
- Partner, Friends, Travel, etc.
- House, Cars, Insurance, etc.
- Dr Appts, Medications, Personal Health, etc.

If you are mentally prepared, keeping your personal issues separate from the customers' issues is easier. If you cannot keep them separate, it will feel like you never get a break. If you can, deal with things before work. Try to put them aside until the end of your workday or on break.

Regulated Industries

In regulated industries, like finance or health care, regulations, rates, and policies change, and you must stay up-to-date. To be prepared, you should read all daily updates and know who to contact if you need help with the changes.

Usually, their computer systems will require multiple steps for authentication and timeout regularly. It will take you longer to prepare at the beginning of the day.

If you were not logged into your systems before you had the customer on the line, it could be 5-10 minutes before you could start helping the customer. This can be very uncomfortable for both you and the customer, and it can make them more upset if you have a demanding customer.

What should I put on my checklist?

To get your checklist started, here are some questions to ask:

How are you going to write things down?
- Digital notepad or pen and paper?
- Do we have a backup pen or pencil?

Are your devices ready?

- Are they powered on, plugged in, and charged?
- Is it working correctly? If not, begin troubleshooting.
- Do you have a backup plan in case the device fails?
- Do you have access to all the necessary networks, like phone, internet, and VPN?
- Do you have a charging cable or replacement batteries for your devices?

What are the main problems customers are going to have today?

- Are you ready to deal with it?
- Do you understand the processes?
- Do you have all the information you need to answer customer questions?

How are you going to track issues and feedback?

- Will you record it in a digital notepad, spreadsheet, or notebook?
- How will you mark it as resolved or needs follow-up?

Add your job-specific items to your checklist so you remember everything.

Notes:

Develop and Maintain Core Skills

"I don't know what that means."

Sometimes, I felt pretty stupid when customers and coworkers used a term or phrase I did not know. I started looking them up using Google. After I got into the habit of doing this, I became more confident when a customer said something I didn't understand and started looking it up while on the call. Knowing what customers were trying to say really built my confidence.

Talking to customers through chat and email is not the same as over the phone

I was good at talking on the phone, but I needed to improve at communicating through text when writing emails and working in chat. I had to learn how to phrase things and practice my typing skills. I spent time watching my coworkers and searching for books, articles, posts, etc., which taught me better communication methods over text. After I developed that skill, my average handle time decreased by 2 minutes, and my CSAT score increased by 12%.

"Did you get an error?" versus "Will you tell me what happened?"

When I was a new rep, I had to ask my customers many questions to get the information I needed from them. Most of my questions could be answered with either yes or no. When I needed more information from a customer, it was hard to get it because they would only answer "Yes" or "No."

My coach always suggested asking an open-ended question, which I thought I was. After listening to other reps, I realized I didn't know what an open-ended question was. So, I started writing down the open-ended questions the other providers were using and started using them, too.

We were not teaching them any basic skills

When I started as a trainer, I noticed that many people who went through my classes had never worked in a customer service job before. They struggled with knowing what to say, so getting on the phone and leading the conversation was very difficult. The training manual I was given did not dedicate time to providing the new agents with these skills, so I decided to develop some lessons and incorporate them into my training classes.

I developed lessons on how to answer calls and greet customers, apologize and show empathy, be patient when a customer is frustrated and more. I saw everyone's skills in my classes improve, even the agents who had done customer service for years. Some of them even thanked me for taking the time to teach these skills during training because they had never been taught them before, and found that they were feeling more confident even though they have been providing service for years.

I received a lot of feedback from the coaches and advisors. The trainees from my classes seemed more prepared and ready to take calls than those from other classes.

What Is "Develop and Maintain Core Skills"?

Core skills are the base skills that you use every day to communicate. To type, read, write, empathize, listen, be patient, etc. These skills are required to understand your customers and to be able to communicate your message. We call them "Core Skills."

You should continuously develop these skills and maintain your skill level—you want it to be as high as possible. These skills are the backbone of providing excellent service and great experiences. Here is a list of some core customer service skills, in no particular order.

- Empathy
- Adaptability
- Use positive language
- Communication Skills
    - Voice (phone)
    - Visual (video chat, in person)
    - Text (email, chat, social media)
- Recognize a question vs statement
- Self-Control
- Responsibility
- Patience
- Emotional maturity
- Listening
- Time management
- Multitasking

We can add many skills to this list, and if you think of others, add them to your list to keep them up to date. We have included skills used in every industry and at every job level. This list contains only some skills you need to provide excellent service.

All these skills are essential, but our communication skills must be maintained at the highest levels possible.

Why It's Important

As providers, we deal with many people daily, which involves a lot of talking, typing, and writing. It also requires problem-solving, multitasking, and exposure to people's emotions. Developing these skills makes you better in all of these areas. When you are good at something, it becomes easier to do.

These skills are essential to providing great experiences. Many will help you throughout your day, especially during back-to-back interactions. They will give you the most benefits during difficult interactions. You will have more confidence during the interaction and be calm and professional.

These skills will help you stay calm and respond politely when a customer says something rude or express your concern when a customer tells you a heartbreaking story.

When a customer provides inappropriate details regarding their personal life or tries to change the subject, they will help you remain professional and redirect the conversation back to the business topic.

When you are having a bad day, they will help you continue to provide great experiences.

Being promoted to an advisor, team leader, coach, or even higher will require dealing with the most challenging situations that will arise. If you have the confidence to handle these situations, you will be an ideal candidate for these promotions.

> ### Hard Definition:
> We must develop and maintain the core skills necessary to provide customer service.

How To "Develop and Maintain Core Skills"

Go through the list of skills, rate yourself on a scale of 1 - 10, and keep track of any skills you still need to learn. For each skill, choose a goal and the rating you would like to achieve. Make a plan to develop the skills you don't have first, then pick your lowest-rated skill and work on it. Make time to work on each skill until your ratings reach your goals.

I have taken multiple courses on communication skills, primarily speaking and writing. Some have been through colleges, continuous education programs, online, and from independent consultants. The skills and techniques I have learned have been used throughout my career.

There are many online courses for developing these core skills; you may also be able to find in-person training locally. Many colleges, universities, etc., offer classes anyone can take, even if they are not students. Many community centers, state and local government, non-profits, career development programs, etc., will offer courses you can take.

Many companies will reimburse tuition for any training or education related to your job or career choice. Ask your team leaders for more training on a specific skill; they may have resources you need to learn about.

Use the time during team meetings to work with your teammates and any scheduled training time. You can also do this during downtime and on your own time.

I learned most of my core skills from my coworkers. When I got my first job in customer service, I needed to improve my communication skills. I was always listening to my neighbors; most of the time, I just copied them. Some would help me and explain why they would say things a certain way. They would listen to me and provide tips; I learned so much during the first year. I am now a very confident communicator on the phone, through email, and by text.

Notes:

Develop and Maintain Core Skills

Record and Resolve Issues

Check, Check, Check

One of the best things I do is write down each issue the customer gives me, and then I work through that list until they are all checked off. I love being able to say, "I can help you solve that," and at the end of the interaction, say, "I was able to solve this and this and this ... Is there anything else?"

I started doing this after I interacted with a customer who started listing everything they wanted help with as soon as I answered the call. I had a hard time keeping up with them. When they finally stopped talking, I did not remember everything they said, so I started with the issues I did remember. After I fixed the first few issues, I asked the customer what else I could help with. I could tell they were a little frustrated that I did not remember everything, but I remembered most of it. They repeated the last two issues, and I worked on those. Ultimately, their frustration was gone, and they thanked me for my help.

I have been writing down every issue ever since.

Promotion Opportunity

Because I made lists of the issues our customers contacted us about and compiled the results, I could find the patterns and most common problems that affected our customers.

I wrote them down and presented them to my manager. They were able to work on implementing fixes for the problems. I did this at two companies I worked for, and in both cases, I got promoted because of my work on our customers' issues.

What is "Record and Resolve Issues"?

An issue is any problem, question, concern, dispute, or matter the customer mentions.

What is an issue?

- *A vital or unsettled matter*
- *Concern, problem*
- *A matter that is in dispute between two or more parties*

Merriam-Webster

Record every issue they mention and try to resolve it.

Have you ever ended an interaction and said to yourself, "I forgot to do this…" or "Did I take care of everything they said?" This happened to us all the time, and it made us realize we needed a way to record every issue they mentioned and mark them as resolved or completed once we had addressed them.

Why It's Important

Recording the customer's issues will help you ensure you resolve all of their problems during your interaction. The list can keep you on track, and you can work through them individually until you are finished. The list will be a great resource when recapping what you did for them.

When issues arise that you cannot solve yourself, you can address them and tell the customer their options to resolve them.

Recording the issues will show your customers that you care because you "remembered" all of them. They will feel like you have listened to their concerns and are serious about helping them. This will lead to complete customer satisfaction and increase your customer satisfaction ratings.

Hard Definition:

We must record every issue the customer reports and attempt to resolve as many issues as possible.

For any issue you cannot resolve during the interaction, explain the next steps of the process and what the customer should expect.

How To "Record and Resolve Issues"

Write down every issue, even the small and simple ones. After you have recorded the issues, you can start to resolve them. Resolve as many issues as you can during this interaction. For any issues we cannot resolve during this interaction, tell the customer what comes next and what to expect.

> *I started by making checklists for what the customer needed help with. Once I knew what they needed help with, I made checklists for what I needed to do to complete each issue. I then went through each checklist and reviewed it with the customer. This ensured I remembered all the steps and resolved their issues. It also makes it easier to tell the customer what we completed at the end of the call.*

It is important to find a way that works for you. Use whatever tools are available to you.

> *I have used Notepad, Word, Google Docs, Sticky Notes, and Google Keep. I make a list as the customer tells me their issues. I type one after the other. Then, I go back through the list and put the capital "I" next to the issues.*

Here are some examples:

```
Needs to update address = I
Make a payment: I


I = Need a refund
I: Reset password
```

When you are finished, you can cross it off the list, put a checkmark next to it, or mark it with an X to signify it is resolved.

Assign A Priority

Assign a priority to help you determine which issues must be solved first or even escalated. Use a higher priority when a customer says, "This is the most important," or "I've called about this three times." Use the '*' asterisk or '!' exclamation point to signify importance.

If possible, keep in touch with the customer until the issue is resolved. Contact them afterward to ensure they have received the resolution and to confirm it has resolved their issue. If not, create another issue and repeat it until it is resolved.

Common Issues

- Change my address
- Forgot my password
- Change credit card
- Request refund
- Lost package
- Damaged item
- Can't log in to the website or app
- Cancel subscription

This will show your customers you care, especially when things go wrong. It will help you create a great experience in a bad situation and lead to complete customer satisfaction.

Long-Term Benefits

You will stand out to your leader as someone who values the customer's experience and wants to contribute to making improvements by recognizing where problems occur and who goes above and beyond their job duties to provide extraordinary service.

Keep this list of the issues and solutions so you can reference it next time you have an issue and see what you did to solve it.

At the end of each work day or week, give your list to your coach, manager, boss, etc., so they can choose what to do with the issues.

Some companies have a dedicated system to record issues. If yours does, use their system, as well. It will help your company find common problems and resolutions faster.

Compliance & Regulations

How do I record issues in an industry where you cannot save data? Work with your team leader or compliance officer, and find a way to record them without saving personal or confidential information.

Notes:

Record and Resolve Issues

Record and Reply To Feedback

Why does everyone keep saying that?

I noticed that many of the customers I spoke to every day were commenting on how hard it was to use our website. It didn't seem difficult to me, so I usually just apologized and tried to help them navigate the website. I started to track how many times customers mentioned it was hard to use. I also started to think about the steps I gave them and realized there was a simpler way to explain them.

I started using the new approach while helping customers, and it worked very well. I would never have thought to change how I explained it if I had not tracked how many times they said it was hard.

Tracking feedback leads to change

I recognized that the agents on my team were starting to mention that the customers were complaining about the same thing over and over. I mentioned this to my manager, but they did not seem to take it very seriously. They said, "Customers complain about a lot of things. I'm sorry. There is nothing I can really do about it. Just apologize to the customer and help them get around it."

I have heard this response from management many times in my years of customer service, but it did not sit well with me this time. I wanted to do something about it, so I started having the agents on my team keep track of the feedback they were getting from our customers. I also got the help of other team leaders and their agents.

After three weeks of tracking, I was able to compile a report that showed exactly how often customers were complaining or providing feedback about these situations and how much it was costing us not to fix the issues. I took this report to my manager's manager and explained that we could not afford to keep getting this negative feedback from our customers. After one look at the report, they agreed, and to my surprise, the company implemented a company-wide fix for the problem.

What Is "Record and Reply To Feedback"?

Record your customer's feedback during your interactions and reply to each one. It's that simple. Replying to their feedback will create a great experience, even if you can't change anything.

> What is feedback?
>
> - Advice, criticism, or information about how good or useful something or somebody's work is.
>
>   Oxford Dictionary
>
> - Helpful information or criticism given to someone to say what can be done to improve a performance, product, etc.
>
>   Britannica

Although simple, this best practice is about more than just saying, "I will submit that feedback for you" or "Thank you for your feedback". Every bit of feedback you hear from the customer is important to them. If you write it down and reply, especially negative feedback, you will create a great experience in a bad situation.

If your customer says, "I don't like using your app," apologize and ask more questions to find out why. Offer to walk them through it so they feel more comfortable or show them a faster way. If you cannot help them or they are not satisfied, pass their feedback on to your leadership.

This definition applies perfectly to customer service industry feedback. It is any information your customer gives you about the business, products, people, website, marketing, features, how things work, etc. As customer service providers, we need to reply to this feedback.

Record any feedback you get, even if it seems small or irrelevant.

Why It's Important

Knowing what customers think is vital to providing great experiences. The information you receive from customers about your service will show you how to improve. Your customers will feel heard and appreciate that you take them seriously.

Report the feedback to your leadership to help them find and fix problems faster.

Replying to their feedback shows them you heard what they said. Your job is to make the customers feel heard and that their opinions matter. Your attention to them will increase the quality of the customer's experience and the likelihood of more business.

> **Hard Definition:**
>
> We must record each piece of feedback the customer provides. Reply to each piece of feedback and attempt to resolve any issues during the same interaction.
>
> Report any feedback about the company to your leadership.

How To "Record and Reply to Feedback"

Keep a pencil and paper with you while interacting with customers. Write down any feedback you receive about products, services, the store, our website, or anything else.

Reply directly to the customer. Thank them for providing the feedback and do anything you can to improve their experience immediately.

Feedback can be received during phone calls, text messages, social media posts, surveys, etc. It can come from anywhere at any time.

Try to collect the following:

- Title
- Priority
- Description
- First Affected Date

Record how the customer was affected and why. Write down any feedback they give us, even if it may seem irrelevant. Record all details of what occurred and how you replied to the feedback.

Report all feedback to your leadership, whether they use it or not.

Keep a list of all the feedback received. Use this list to identify repeat comments, likes, dislikes, etc. When a customer provides similar feedback, look at this list for any solutions you can provide. Report this list to your leadership. Use it to stand out, get a promotion, get a raise, etc.

You will stand out to your leaders as someone who values customers' opinions and goes above and beyond their job duties to provide outstanding service.

If you can't answer these questions, ask your leadership:
- Where should you report feedback as an employee?
- Where can customers report feedback besides reporting it to you?
- What happens to that feedback?
- Does the customer get a response as a result?

DIY example

If your employer does not provide a solution to record feedback, create one yourself. It will help your experiences surpass others and increase your customer satisfaction ratings.

If you have email, send yourself an email every time it happens, then save those emails in a separate folder. You can use this method to record the date and time of the occurrence without recording any personal, proprietary, or protected information.

Notes:

Record and Reply To Feedback

Practice, Practice, Practice

I want to max out my bonus money

I have played baseball since I was five and started playing in competitive leagues when I was 10. My coaches always held practices between our games 2-3 times a week. That taught me how much I could improve my skills by repeatedly practicing drills.

When I started working in customer service, I wanted to be the best and get the biggest bonus possible. So, I practiced specific scenarios over and over, even between phone calls, like running drills at baseball practice. This helped me become comfortable dealing with these situations.

After I was comfortable with almost every situation, I could max out my bonuses almost every month, and some months, I got 100% QAs and CSAT!

It doesn't seem like practice, but it is working.

I had a team leader who liked to quiz us. She loved asking the hard questions to see how well we understood the policies and procedures. She would also give us fake scenarios and ask, "How would you respond?" I love it, and I love coming up with clever answers to her challenging scenarios. I kept feeling more and more confident talking to customers, even when the situations were complicated.

I never thought of it as practice; it was more like a game, but it helped me practice talking to customers and dealing with weird situations. It showed me how important it is to practice anything I am struggling with or uncomfortable with.

Flashcards, just like at school

My coworkers always asked me how I got so good at answering customers' questions. I would create flashcards with a question a customer might ask on the front and possible answers on the back. Then, I would spend time going through them between calls. Sometimes, my neighbors would join in, and we would quiz each other. That was my best trick and always seemed to work for me.

During calls, if I get a question I can't immediately answer, I write it down. After the call, I will create a flash card and start practicing. My coworkers always give me questions to make into flash cards. We have built up a lot of cards, but we can always grab a handful and start practicing.

What Is "Practice, Practice, Practice"?

The definition of this best practice is literally in the name: practice, practice, and practice some more. Practice makes us feel confident and comfortable doing things. It makes us feel strong and capable of doing a good job. It also ensures we do it right.

Practice needs to happen regularly, possibly every day. Practice until you feel confident completing the task or process on your own.

Why It's Important

> *Practice does not make perfect. Practice makes permanent. Repeat the same mistakes over and over, and you don't get any closer to Carnegie Hall.*
>
> *Sarah Kay*

You must be comfortable and confident when interacting with customers, regardless of the circumstances. When you are not confident handling the interaction, you will struggle to provide great experiences.

Practice creates "muscle memory" or "instinct". This will allow us to be ready for any situation. You can focus on the customer and help in any way possible.

It will help to ensure you remember how to do it in moments of stress or panic. Customers may contact us during stressful situations; sometimes, we can be caught off guard and panicked. We can still be confident and work through difficult interactions. The trick is to practice before it comes up so you are ready.

> **Hard Definition:**
> We must practice as much as possible. Practice until you are confident you can handle any interaction.

How To "Practice, Practice, Practice"

Define scenarios to practice. Use your "How To" to find scenarios. Your employer may have practice scenarios defined and available for your use. Outline what roles are involved and explain the details of the situation.

Each scenario should include any possible outcomes, as well as a script for the customer and one for the provider.

Practice these scenarios as often as possible to feel comfortable handling the scenario on our own.

Schedule a time to practice every week. During this time, use the scenarios you defined for practice. Pick a scenario and follow the directions to act out that interaction with a customer or prospect.

Practice different scenarios for each process you have. Use scenarios that match the ones you deal with every day. The more accurate you make the scenario, the better it will prepare you to deal with real customers.

Try to practice situations you may not encounter daily. These scenarios will be the most challenging since you need more experience dealing with them. If you practice them, you will gain more knowledge and be ready. Find someone who has done it before and learn what they did.

Practice until you are comfortable and confident. Take advantage of any opportunity to practice new experiences and tasks.

Example Scenario

A customer requests to waive the past due fee.
Define dates, amounts, times, etc, for when the payment was made.
Define if the provider can waive the fee and why or why not.

Questions To Ask When Defining Scenarios

What scenarios do I need to practice?
What areas do I need to practice most?
What goals do I want to achieve?
What areas did I miss on my QA evaluations?

During training, practice the scenarios as many times as possible. Practicing is more critical than any other aspect of training.

Push Yourself To Get Even Better

In the first few scenarios, you should have scripts to follow for both sides, the customer and the provider. After the first 2-5 practice runs, depending on the subject matter, the scripts should be condensed into outlines of what the customer needs and a checklist of what will need to be completed during the scenario.

At this point, the scenarios should test your knowledge and ability to do it independently.

After five practice runs like this, you should move on to an outline for the person playing the customer and no script for yourself. You should feel comfortable talking with the customer and know how to use the systems and resources to perform your job.

Try to formulate your responses and look for the answers.

Track Your Progress

Record the practice, review the recordings, and rate yourself. Keep trying until you are meeting your goals.

Use the time between interactions and during your team meetings to practice with your coworkers. Learn their techniques and practice applying them to your interactions. Use the time during 1-on-1 meetings to listen to other providers. If you need it, ask your team leader for more training time to practice.

Take some time before and after your shift to practice. Ask some friends and family to pretend to be customers.

Notes:

Practice, Practice, Practice

Providing Service

This section will teach you the best practices you will use while providing service. Providing excellent service will require you to be open to learning about yourself and honest with yourself about what you are doing right and what you are doing wrong.

It requires you to be dedicated, consistent, and professional. You must be willing to learn about yourself, admit your mistakes, and learn from them. You also have to be willing to learn from others and ready to practice.

- Always Use "How To"
- Answer Confidently
- Write Everything Down
- Be Polite
- Communicate Clearly
- Listen to Understand
- Be A Guide
- Same Way Every Time
- The Power of "Oh ..."
- Don't Judge
- Avoid Negativity
- Reset Button
- Use Recovery Time

Always Use "How To"

I found the answer on my own

I felt so stupid when a process changed and I didn't know about it. Using "How To" allowed me to act like "I knew what I was doing" the whole time, even though I had to look it up. I am always confident in my ability to solve any problem a customer has.

Last week, they said something different. You don't know what you are doing.

A customer called in and asked a complicated question. I tried to answer it from memory but did not get it right. The customer said angrily, "I called last week, and they said I could do that. You don't know what you are doing!" They asked for a supervisor. I was worried I would get in trouble once the supervisor found out, and I struggled for the rest of the day.

The worst thing you can do is offer a solution that is not available.

I work at a pharmacy, and our medications are only available through home delivery. A customer called in because they did not receive their delivery. They were very upset and concerned because they were almost out of the medication. I was trying to hurry and reassured them we could send a replacement. I went through the process of refunding their copay and reversing the claim with their insurance, but when it came time to send the replacement, I could not create it because their prescription was out of refills. We would have to get a new prescription from their doctor, which can take 4-10 days.

Our "How To" says to check the prescription before offering options. If I had been following the process in "How To," I would have been able to tell the customer upfront that we would have to get a new prescription. Instead, they expected me to send a replacement, but I could not. When I explained that to the customer, they became furious and asked for a supervisor.

Turns out, I was wrong

Most of the time, I just went off of my memory for how to complete tasks. I have been working here for three years and am very familiar with our processes. Once, a customer called me out for being wrong about a process.

It turns out they completed this transaction one or two times every month, so they were very familiar with the process. I was wrong, and they were right.

At that point, I apologized for being incorrect and offered to complete the transaction for them, but by this point, they were pretty upset. They said they did not trust me to do it correctly and asked if they could speak to my supervisor. After the interaction, I felt terrible for being wrong and wasting the customer's time.

The supervisor who took the call contacted my supervisor, and I was written up. After that interaction, I started using my "How To" on every call, even when I thought I knew how to do it correctly.

What Is "Always Use How To"?

As customer service providers, we must ensure we are doing things right. We do not want to give a customer incorrect information or set the wrong expectations; this will always create a bad experience, and we can face consequences with our employer. If you work in a regulated industry, you may face harsher consequences.

What is a "How To"?

A "How To" is a group of documents with information about completing all tasks for your job position. It is the source of truth you should use to know how to perform tasks, what steps to follow in specific situations, and what rules apply and when.

You may have heard it called a knowledge base, information center, manual, or policies and procedures.

Ideally, there should be written, step-by-step instructions for each procedure or task you may need to complete while interacting with customers. Not all employers have a "How To," so we will teach you ways to apply this best practice when they don't.

Why It's Important

When you have a question about how to complete a task or the rules in this specific scenario, make this the first place you look. You will save time because you will not have to scramble to find the answer. You will also ensure that you follow the process correctly and that the customer gets all the necessary information.

If you use "How To," you can be confident you did it right. You will have higher QA and compliance scores because you followed the process step by step, didn't miss anything, checked all the criteria, and explained the required information.

You will have more satisfied customers, and they will give you higher customer satisfaction (CSAT) scores.

Following "How-To" will increase your efficiency when performing complex tasks. It will help you stay on track and keep your place. It will help you learn how to do your job faster. It is great to rely on in moments of stress and confrontation.

> **Hard Definition:**
>
> Use your "How To" during every interaction and for each task. Always check for updates and follow the directions, tips, or advice included.
>
> If your "How To" is missing something or is incorrect, report it to your team leader.
>
> Keep your own "How To" and document anything you need to complete tasks. Include tips, warnings, important phone numbers or addresses, etc. Anything that will simplify your day or keep you compliant.

How To "Always Use How To"

When a customer tells you their issue, write it down and search for it in "How-To". Even if you know the answer, search "How To" for every issue to build a habit. This will ensure nothing has changed since the last time you used the "How To" document.

> *I love that I can open a browser tab for each article and policy. I leave the tabs open all day, and I have a folder of bookmarks for the ones I open daily. It saves me so much time, and it is so easy.*

Almost all the mistakes I made were when I thought I didn't need to use "How To" and didn't even look at it. I make a lot fewer mistakes when I pull up the task.

You need to use it during every interaction, every time. You should not go off memory alone. Everything will change eventually. You should review the task to ensure everything has stayed the same and check for unusual circumstances.

You must decide to do this during every interaction and then stick to it. After you have worked at the same place for a while, you start to memorize every situation. This is when you will need help with this practice. You may begin to feel like there is no point because the process has stayed the same and will stay the same for a while. Even if it might not change, pull it up anyway. This is where you will make a mistake and regret it.

When it feels like you don't need to pull up "How To" anymore, adjust your strategy. Instead of using it on every interaction, pull it up on the first interaction of the day, check back a few times to ensure everything has stayed the same, and verify you completed all the necessary steps.

Regulated Industries

Many procedures in these industries are regulated and must be followed exactly to ensure compliance. Following "How To" will guide you and ensure you do not make any mistakes. Policies, procedures, and regulations can change frequently, and using "How To" for every interaction ensures you have the most up-to-date instructions.

Some procedures must be followed verbatim for compliance reasons, but you should use the "How To" as a guide throughout your day.

Make sure you use your how-to for complicated and detailed situations, such as releasing pending payments, a COVID payment agreement, applications, changes@ in terms, etc.

Every time I went into my local bank to do a balance transfer, the person I talked to had no idea what I was talking about or how to do it. In 2022, they still could not do it online, so I had to go into the branch. The teller would have to find someone and ask them how to do it.

There were two tellers who knew how to do it. One day, I asked them what they had to do so I could tell the person the next time I came in. They said the code was "bal.tran" and then they filled out the form. It was that simple.

I saved it on my phone so I would not forget. The next time I went in, it was a new teller who did not know how to do it, but I did. I could not believe my bank did not have a manual for employees to look at such a simple thing.

Build Your Own "How To"

If your employer does not have a "How To," ask for one. If they cannot provide one, you can create your own and document the processes as you were taught. Use this resource as your "How To" to ensure you complete tasks correctly.

Whenever you ask questions about a task, add the situation and answer to your "How To" document. Write down the date you got that answer, and who gave it so you always have the most up-to-date information.

Use a simple text document or spreadsheet. Give the problem a title and brief description. Then, write down the steps to resolve the issue. Include links and templates where possible.

Even if your employer does provide a "How To," you can still create your own cheat sheets with tips, reminders, shortcuts, etc., to make finding the answers you are looking for easier.

Examples

In Notepad, I saved a file for each category of tasks to keep the number of files small. Then, I created a Title for each task and used a dashed line to separate each task. To search, I used the find feature ctrl+f (control+f).

In Google Docs, I created a folder for each category type and a document for each task. Each document had a title that described the task. To search, I used the search feature at the top of Google Drive; this allowed me to explore the content of the documents and the titles to find what I needed.

I can't write anything down

If you cannot write things down and save information, devise a creative way to do it. Be sure you are following your employer's rules and not putting your job at risk. Ask your coach if you could type it up and have them print and laminate it for you.

Possible Promotion or Job Opportunity

Some companies do not have someone to maintain their "How To." It may be left up to team leaders or management, but they often do not have the time.

If your company does not have a "How To" or is consistently outdated, this can be an opportunity for a promotion. We have had multiple trainees use this to create a new position, maintaining their "How To," and many received raises.

If you are interested in this kind of position, prepare a report detailing how you can help the company be more efficient, stay compliant, and make fewer errors. Explain how it will help all their providers and how you can keep it current.

Notes:

Always Use "How To"

Answer Confidently

They don't believe me

During a one-on-one with my coach, they asked if anything had been bothering me. I said, "Customers don't believe me! They always ask me, 'Are you sure?' or 'Will you check again?' I know I am giving the right answer, but they never believe it."

We listened to a few of my calls, and my coach pointed out that on one call, I said, "Umm...the cutoff time is noon," and the customer replied, "Are you sure?" On another call, I said, "I think it was on time...yes, it was on time," and again, the customer replied, "Are you sure?"

They suggested I pause before answering any questions and, if I am sure of the answer, don't say "umm..." or "I think..."; just give them the answer. I put a sticky note on my screen that says, "If you know the answer, don't say umm..." This has been working really well, and customers don't ask me if I am sure anymore.

I felt stupid and uncomfortable not knowing the answers to customer's questions

When I was new, I always felt stupid when I didn't know the answer, and it was awkward trying to cover it up until I found it. One of my coworkers always said, "I will have to do some research, just one moment." I started copying them, and it helped build trust with the customer and gave me plenty of time to find the correct answer.

I say the same thing as you; why doesn't it work for me?

A coworker once said to me, "I say the same thing as you, but people never believe me. They always say, 'Are you sure?' and sometimes ask for a supervisor. Why is that?" They sat pretty close to me, so I started listening to what they were saying, but they did not seem very confident. They hesitated when answering or began by saying, "I think...". I explained that they wouldn't say, "I think..." if they knew the answer. This is what was causing the customer to doubt their answer.

When I don't know the answer, I always say, "It may take me a few minutes to find out for you. Can you hold for me, please?" When I find the answer, I take some time to practice saying it before I take the customer off hold so I feel confident in what I am going to say.

Because I took the time to look up the answer, I am more confident in what I am about to tell them, which makes it less tempting to say "I think" or "umm." When I return to the customer, I say, "Here is what I found out," and then give them the information.

What Is "Answer Confidently"?

While interacting with customers, you will be asked a variety of questions. Some you will know the answer right away, others you will have to research, and some you may have never been asked. This can be intimidating, especially if they catch you by surprise.

You should respond confidently to a customer's question, even when you don't know the answer. Just because you don't know the answer right away does not mean you don't know what you are doing. Even though some customers can make you feel under pressure, you can always take time to find the answer.

You can be confident you will be able to find the answer.

Why It's Important

It will show your willingness to help, regardless of the situation. Tell the customer you will find out, and you can be comfortable doing the research. You won't feel rushed and can take the time necessary to get the correct answer, reducing stress and mistakes.

Customers will either work with you or against you. Many are defensive and prepared to fight for what they need. You establish yourself as an authority or expert when you give a confident answer. The customer will feel comfortable and start working with you instead of against you.

Customers will trust your answers and believe in your ability to help. They will feel comfortable asking more questions and getting the help they need.

If the customer trusts you, they will be more willing to wait for the correct answer. They are even willing to call back or wait for a call back in a few days as long as they know they will get the correct answer. This trust will also reduce transfers, escalations, and callbacks.

> **Hard Definition:**
>
> We must always provide a confident answer, even when we don't know. We can be confident that we will find the correct answer.
>
> We must always greet our customers confidently at the beginning of each interaction.

How To "Answer Confidently"

If a customer asks a question and you don't know the answer, always give them a confident response and then find the answer.

- "I would be happy to check that for you. Can you hold for a few minutes, please?"
- "That is a great question. Can you give me a few minutes to look that up?"

It may take a few seconds or a few minutes to find. Let them know you are searching for the correct answer, which will take a few minutes. Check-in with the customer and set realistic expectations about how long it might take.

Once you have found the answer, start to prepare your response. Take your time and find the right way to present the information so the customer will understand.

My ability to answer confidently comes from my confidence in myself and my abilities. No matter the customer's question, I want to help and am willing to find the answer. This is what gave me the confidence I needed to be able to answer any customer's question.

Plan phrases for different situations and practice saying them until they feel comfortable. This will make your responses feel natural.

Say something like this:

- "I would be happy to check that for you. "
- "Give me just a moment to check that for you".
- "That is a great question; let me see what I can find out for you".

Your response is 100% confident, and you have yet to answer. The great thing about this response is you sound like you know what you are doing, even though you don't have the answer yet. Your customers will be confident you will try to help them.

Pace And Tone

Use tone and speed to help you achieve this. Say it with a warm, friendly, positive attitude, and like you mean it. Take deep breaths to help you calm your heart rate, and avoid speaking fast because you are nervous.

When you have a message to deliver, say it as a statement, not a question. If you say it as a question, you are asking them if this information is okay, not giving them the answer to their question.

Don't Use Filler

Don't hesitate to ask them to hold if you need more time. Never guess, give false information, or give partial answers. You will cause more harm, and the customer will need to contact you again to get the correct answer. Always do the research and then answer confidently. Don't try to answer while researching; you will sound distracted and unsure.

Have defined phrases or scripts for each interaction so you have multiple ways to respond. This will help you avoid filler words such as um, okay, and like. During your scheduled training time, practice answering the most challenging questions that customers ask us.

In Person

If you are in person, don't be concerned that they can see you doing the research. This will build their trust in you. If you need to leave the customer alone for a moment, tell them you will be right back and how long you will be gone.

Customers will stop you to ask where to find a specific item. If you are not confident about where the item is, you can still answer confidently by saying, "I am not sure, but I will help you find it." Always stop what you are doing and work with the customer until the item is found. Avoid giving them partial directions or saying where you think it is; it will cause confusion and doubt.

Regulated Industries

Some industries are highly regulated, like credit cards or health care. If you work in a regulated industry, your answers to customers must be accurate and precise. Some answers require you to follow a specific script, or you could cause harm to a customer.

When you visit the doctor, you expect confident and knowledgeable help. Credit card customers are very concerned about their finances and credit card costs. These customers expect you to know what you are talking about.

It is best to double-check the answer, even if it takes longer. Your customers need to trust the information you give them. Otherwise, they will have a horrible experience.

New Product/Service Or Policy

When a new product, service, or policy change is introduced, make a list of all the questions customers might ask and then think of ways to respond.

Bad News

You will have to deliver bad news to customers and brainstorm ways to respond to their reactions and questions. Give the bad news directly, don't beat around the bush, and be as straightforward as possible. It is even worse to deliver the bad news again.

Example Phrases:

"Give me just a moment to check that for you."
"That is a good question. I will find out for you."
"I would be happy to see what I can find out for you."
"No one has ever asked me that before. Give me just a moment to find out."

Practice:

Work with a partner, challenge each other with hard questions, and practice answering when you don't know the answer. Ask a question they will not know the answer to. It does not have to be anything associated with our job or industry.

They should respond by telling you they don't know and asking you to hold while they look up the answer. They should then search for the answer and respond confidently.

Try these questions:

- How tall is the Empire State Building?
- How tall is the Eiffel Tower?
- What is the population of the USA in 2022?
- What is the square root of 2478?
- How much does the International Space Station weigh?
- What is the speed of light?
- How big is the Indian Ocean?
- What is the longest road in the US?
- How many permanent seats does the Indianapolis Motor Speedway in Indiana, USA have?
- What is the melting point of Magnesium?
- How many seconds are there in 6 days?

When you give your answers to the questions above, look up the answers first so you know you are correct, then practice saying them over and over until you feel confident. Then, do this same thing with the questions from your customers.

Notes:

Answer Confidently

Write Everything Down

I always feel stupid asking a customer to repeat themselves.

I have forgotten to write down what the customer said so many times. I always felt stupid asking them to repeat themselves, especially when I was asking for sensitive information. After feeling that way too many times, I made a goal to write down what they said so I would not have to ask them to repeat it.

Once I built the habit of writing everything down, I felt more competent, and I was always able to surprise customers because I remembered what they said at the beginning of our interaction.

I clearly remember a call when a customer was in a public area, trying to purchase with their credit card. I had to verify some sensitive info, and they were uncomfortable saying it out loud because they did not want others to hear it. If I had not written it down when they gave it to me the first time, it would have ruined the experience. Because I wrote it down and could repeat it back to them, they became less agitated because they knew it was being kept confidential.

I thought I knew what they were calling about.

I had a phone call with a customer that started like all the others. The customer explained what they needed help with, and I went to work on it. While I was working, they told me about a situation that happened to them a few days earlier. I politely listened to their story. They kept saying, "That was on Tuesday; now it's Friday."

As they continued, they said something that made me realize the customer was telling me about another problem they were having with us, not about some random event earlier in the week.

As soon as I realized it, I asked the customer to repeat the details of the situation. I did not think those details were relevant when they were initially explaining it, so I did not write them down. The customer became angry with me. They yelled at me for not listening to anything they said and demanded to speak with a supervisor.

I felt awful because I did not write those things down. I knew how to solve the problem, but they did not want my help. Because the customer felt disrespected,

I did not have the opportunity to help them. There was also a chance I would get a low QA score or get in trouble for what happened.

I decided to write down all the details the customer provided, even if it did not seem relevant. I am happy to say I never found myself in that situation with a customer again, and it is because I write everything down.

Surprise a Customer

My call started as a regular call about making a payment and asking for a past-due fee waived. So I was writing down all the details that she had given me. As the call went on, she started talking about how she was working out of town for a few months, and she was so sad because her father had passed away recently; she was telling me about the things that she was doing to try and cope.

After the call was over, I felt so bad for what she had been going through. I was telling my coach about it, and she reminded me of a program this company had that allowed you to send a gift to a customer if you make a special connection with them, but you have to provide the details of the connection, or they can't fulfill the request (to prevent people from sending gifts to family, and prevent abuse, etc.).

Because I had written down the details of everything she told me, I was able to use my outline to recap what happened. If I had not documented it so well, remembering everything that happened on that call would have been a lot harder.

"I want to make a payment."

An angry customer called many times to make a payment, but the automated system did not take his information. He came into the call distraught and said, "I want to make a payment, my routing number is this ... the account number is this ... and I wanna pay $200.00."

I quickly wrote down the information while he was giving it to me. I replied, "Of course, sir, I would be happy to take care of that for you. Let me make sure I typed those numbers correctly."

If I hadn't written that down, I would never have remembered it all, and he would have been more upset. This call ended on a good note, but others have not.

"My computer restarted, and I lost all my work."

Once, while I was in ACW (after-call work) completing my work for a customer, I noticed that other people were posting messages in our Slack channel that their computer had just restarted without warning, their call had been disconnected, and they had lost all of their work.

I realized the same thing would probably happen to me, so I quickly wrote down the information I needed to finish my work and saved it. About two minutes later, my computer restarted.

I was fortunate in this case because others around me had the problem before I did. The account I was working on at the time had a lot of tickets to submit, and not completing the work would have caused significant harm to the customer.

I felt so relieved that I had the chance to save my work before it was lost. Calling the customer back to redo all the work would have been very stressful for both of us. Usually, I don't save my notes because this sort of thing does not happen, and once I am done with my work, I delete the notes and start over. I think I will start saving from now on.

What Is "Write Everything Down"?

One of the simplest things you can do to provide a great experience is to write everything down. You will be amazed at how much this little trick can help you.

Write down all the information your customers give you about their problems. It seems obvious to write down the necessary details like names, dates, account numbers, order numbers, etc., but you should also write down the details that may not seem important or relevant at the time. If the customer says it, it usually means something to them. These details often come in handy later during your interaction.

Write down all the details as the customer explains their situation. The customer is telling you what happened and what is important to them. You can use this information later to create a great experience.

Why It's Important

It will show you respect the customer and that you are paying attention and taking their issue seriously.

One of the most important things to customers is having their issues solved. Writing down the details will give you a better chance of solving it. It will often provide you with most of the information you need. It is a huge relief to realize you have the necessary information, especially if the interaction has ended.

Not having the information when you need it makes everything harder. It makes you look like you were not paying attention and didn't care about helping this customer.

Don't make customers repeat themselves. Making the customer repeat the same information repeatedly is disrespectful, and they may become upset by it. This is even more important when asking for sensitive information or information during a sensitive moment. Don't make them repeat it unless necessary.

Your customers will be pleasantly surprised when you remember the details that they expected you to forget. It will show you cared enough to remember.

> *After working with a customer for an extended period and reviewing all the details of the situation, the customer was so grateful to hear that I had written it all down so they did not have to repeat it. It was one of those experiences where the customer called several times and had to explain the whole situation repeatedly.*

You will avoid sending a follow-up email or making callbacks to obtain additional information. This will save time and improve the conversation.

Use it to give you power in the conversation. You have the information you need to solve their problem.

Hard Definition:

We must write down all the information the customer gives us so they can avoid repeating themselves. We will use this information throughout the interaction to solve problems and make connections.

How To "Write Everything Down"

Where Are You Going To Write Things Down?:

Start by choosing how you are going to write things down. Will you use paper and pen, word processing documents, electronic notepads, sticky notes, etc?

If you choose a digital option, choose a separate program/system from any work programs/systems. This will prevent you from losing your notes if the production systems fail.

For example, one of my previous employers used a system that timed out every 30 minutes and required you to refresh or log in to keep the system active. When a customer called in, you searched for their account with their phone number. When you typed the phone number into the search and hit enter, the search would not work because the system was inactive, and the phone number was not saved. Now I have to ask the customer for their phone number again.

If I had written the phone number down in my digital notepad instead, I would still have it and could try the search again without making my customers repeat themselves. This is even more beneficial when you would have lost more data than just a phone number.

What Should I Write Down?

Write down anything that helps you remember and create a picture of what is happening. Condense the longer items to a few bullet points that give you enough information to remember what was said.

Write down everything necessary for the experience, issues, and feedback the customer mentions.

- All names, dates, addresses, account numbers, invoices, etc.
- The details of what happened.
- What were they trying to do, and at what step did it occur?

When you think of something you need to tell the customer, write it down so you don't forget to tell them. This will remind you of everything you need to do for the customer.

Sometimes, a customer will talk for a while and mention several things that must be addressed. Making a list ensures you remember to tell them.

Private Or Personal Information

When writing down private and personal information, verify it is correct before proceeding. Avoid making the customer repeat it. People get uncomfortable repeating it, especially in public places.

Interaction Recap

Refer to your list to ensure you have completed everything. At the end of your conversation, recap the list with your customers to ensure you have completed everything they asked for. Example: "We have updated your address and phone number. I requested a replacement card be sent to your new address. Is there anything else I can help you with today?"

Can I Ask Them To Repeat Themselves?

Yes, it is okay to ask a customer to repeat themselves when necessary, like when you did not hear what they said or did not quite understand it. It's not okay to have them repeat themselves because you were not paying attention or did not write it down.

How to ask your customers to repeat themselves:

> *"I'm sorry, I didn't hear everything you said. Could you please repeat it?"*
> *"I didn't quite catch that. Could you say that again, please?"*
> *"I think the phone cut out. Would you please repeat that?"*
> *"I didn't hear that last part. Would you mind repeating it?"*

More Examples of What To Write Down:
- Type of pet and pet's name
- Something of personal interest they mention
- Where they are going this weekend or for vacation
- Their hobbies and interests
- Reason why the item is needed or important to them. Maybe it's a special occasion or something urgent.
- Anything you might need to solve their problem or make a connection later.

Build Rapport, Create Unique Experiences

You can use some of that information to build rapport and unique experiences. For example, you could close the communication by saying, "I hope your puppy Jake gets better soon," or "Have fun at your Aunt's birthday party." This is handy when you need to fill those awkward silence or dead air moments.

When working as a cashier, I keep a pencil and paper next to the register. It is handy when customers say they prefer a different size, color, flavor, or brand. I keep the pencil and paper in my shirt pocket when working on the floor. I don't always have to use it, but I write it down when a customer says they are looking for multiple things or something particular.

Notes:

Be Polite

Kindness kills negativity

I have had many interactions where the customer is very upset right at the beginning of the call. I struggled with these calls because they were always intense; they even made me shake.

I remember one customer was calling because his credit card was not working, and he was on vacation across the country. He was very upset and clearly embarrassed whenever he tried to use his card. No matter what I said, he had an angry response and even started calling me names and threatening to sue the company.

I tried to stay as calm as I could. I had to ask him many questions to determine why the card was not working. Each time he answered, I said, "Thank you," and he calmed down slightly.

Then, I had to ask him to try using the chip at least two more times. When I asked him, he was angry again and said, "You really want me to try again and look foolish?" I said, "If you would, please try it again. I apologize for any embarrassment, but I need to find out if it is the chip." He tried it, but it still didn't work. I asked him to use it again; he replied, "Are you serious? It obviously is not working, and now there is a line of angry people behind me!" I said, "Yes, please try it one more time, and the machine will ask you to swipe the card using the magnetic strip."

He grumbled but tried again. It didn't work, and the machine asked him to swipe the card. He swiped the card, and it worked. He finished his transaction and was walking away from the cashier. He then said, "I am sorry. Thank you for helping me." I said, "You're welcome. I am glad it could help."

I told him I had requested a new card, which would be sent to his house, and that he may have to swipe the card for the rest of the trip. He said again, "Thank you for helping me. I will try swiping the card next t time. I am sorry for being so rude".

The whole conversation turned around because I was polite and patient.

Just say, "I'm sorry".

I remember a situation while I was donating plasma that has stuck with me for a long time. While I was sitting in the waiting area, another customer came in with some required paperwork for her to donate. The person at the desk looked at the paperwork and said, "This is wrong; we don't do this anymore."

The customer said they were told by someone in one of the offices back there while pointing that this was the paperwork they needed and that they would be able to donate once they got the paperwork. They replied, "That is the old way; we don't do that anymore."

It was starting to make me uncomfortable. I said to myself, "Just say I'm sorry," "Just say I'm sorry," over and over, but they never did. You could tell the customer was confused and frustrated, and they explained how much time and effort it took to complete the paperwork.

The employee just kept repeating the same thing over and over again. To make matters worse, two other employees were standing next to them, and neither of them showed any sort of empathy. It was like they all grouped together to prove to the customer that they were right and the customer was wrong. At this point, the customer became furious, and to keep herself from yelling at them, she just said, "Thanks for nothing," and rushed out the door.

I was so put off by this situation that I never returned to that plasma center again, and I wasn't even the customer it happened to.

"I don't want your payment to be late."

While working at a credit card company, I was working with a customer who wanted to make a payment; she was on the train on her way home from work. When I asked for her payment details, she realized she did not have her debit card in her wallet. She apologized and said, "I will call you back when I get home in about 5 minutes".

I quickly jumped in and asked her to wait for a moment. This particular company had a payment deadline of 8 pm on the due date, which I noticed was about 15 minutes away. We also had a hold time of about 10 minutes; if she were to call back later, her payment would be late for sure.

I mentioned this to the customer and explained that I wanted her to avoid getting billed a $35 late fee over such a simple thing. I offered to stay on the line with her until she got home so we could get her payment in on time.

While she walked home, we chatted about her day at work and what we were planning for dinner. She got home 5 minutes later, and we were able to submit her payment 5 minutes before the cut-off time.

She was so grateful for the extra time I had taken and the friendship I had offered. She made sure to thank me for it several times and gave me a great review on my customer satisfaction survey.

Customers will choose excellent service over fast service.

One day, while at the grocery store, I noticed three of the registers only had one customer in line, but the line was much longer at the fourth register. I thought that was odd, so I started watching for a little while to find out why.

At the first three registers with no line, neither of the cashiers said hello to the customer when they got to the register, not even when the customer said hello first. They were not smiling and sounded annoyed when they told the customer their balance. They even seemed upset when no customers were in their line; they just stood there with angry faces. I could tell customers were avoiding them on purpose.

At the fourth register, the one with the long line, the cashier had a completely different demeanor. They said hello to every customer as they got to the register. They made small talk while scanning their groceries and said, "Thank you for shopping with us." One of the customers was a mom with three young children. I could tell the cashier wanted to help because they even offered to have someone come and help her take the groceries to their car. The mother was delighted and said, "Yes, that would be great."

I thought it was amazing that in this world of "get things done as fast as possible," people were willing to wait in a longer line to work with someone polite over someone who was not.

What Is "Be Polite"?

Being polite is more than just saying please and thank you. It is an overall mindset and attitude of respect and kindness, regardless of how the customer acts or what they may say. Be polite throughout the entire communication.

We have noticed that things do not go well when providers are not polite, even in the most basic situations. We have observed it in every industry. Being polite can be one of your most powerful tools in providing great experiences.

Put the customer first. If they interrupt, let them speak first. Be patient and give them time to look up the information you need. Go out of your way to be kind during every interaction.

Why It's Important

Being polite helps create positive feelings for you and the customer. It shows respect and appreciation for them contacting you. Everyone loves to be appreciated, and feeling respected makes your customers feel great.

It will help to create a positive atmosphere, even when customers are upset and negative. It will build trust. It will feel more like they are talking to a friend, and you care about what they say. They will feel more comfortable talking to you and asking questions.

It is harder for a customer to be rude when you are kind. Kindness kills negativity. By the end of the communication, your customers will feel better. They will be more likely to refer their friends and family. And the really bad ones will be less likely to badmouth the company.

No matter how hard the day was, if you are polite, you will feel better at the end of the day.

It shows your customers what kind of treatment they can expect when contacting your company. It will set a great example, and the customers will follow it, even when upset.

It will help de-escalate tense situations. No matter how angry they get, being polite will always help.

> *It seems obvious that you should be polite, but throughout my years in customer service, I have witnessed so many interactions where providers did hardly anything to be polite. They don't say please, thank you, or I'm sorry. Especially when it's obvious that saying "I'm sorry" could turn*

everything around. Don't take these little gestures for granted. They are very powerful when used.

> **Hard Definition:**
>
> We must always be polite and respectful, even in the worst situations. It will always be beneficial.

How To "Be Polite"

Treat every customer with the same level of respect as the last. Treat all customers as if they are the best customers you have ever had, even the bad ones. Continue being polite even when they are not, and rise above it. Remain professional at all times.

Show good manners through your behavior and speech. Try hard not to interrupt while they are speaking. Ask questions kindly and thank them for their answers. Show appreciation for the customer when they help you solve their problem. When you ask a question, always say please. When they give you an answer, say thank you. Be patient; let them take their time.

Do not sigh or huff and puff when a customer interrupts you or asks a question that annoys you. Don't change your tone of voice to be monotone or condescending. You should maintain the same friendly, polite attitude even when annoyed or frustrated.

You need to maintain your positivity, attitude, and mental state. Take deep breaths and stay calm during tense situations.

Smile while you are speaking, even if they can't see you. Use a mirror to keep ourselves smiling. Smile while you write emails or texts; it will help you be happy and more polite.

Offer to wait while they look things up, help their kids, answer the door, or take another call.

Put your customers first. Make sure they understand the message you are trying to convey. Say please every time you ask for something, and thank them every time they give you something you asked for.

Whenever a customer interrupts or speaks at the same time you do, stop speaking and let the customer talk.

In-Person Interactions

Greet every customer as they enter and every customer who approaches you for help. Chat with every customer who tries to start a conversation.

When a customer asks you for help, stop what you are doing and help them, even if it means going to the other side of the store.

Look for as many opportunities to help as possible. Watch for customers who need help reaching an item or have their arms full and may need help carrying their items. Offer to reach the item for them, get them a basket, or even help bring some items to the register.

Offer additional assistance to anyone who seems to need help. Offer to help load groceries into the car, assist those in need with shopping, hold umbrellas, and walk customers to their vehicles during a storm.

Kindness kills negativity; politeness kills rudeness.

What should I do? The customer is still upset and being rude.

Keep your tone calm and polite while maintaining the same pace. Pause for a moment before replying to questions and responses. Don't go monotone or sound judgmental.

It is hard, but you can treat them the same way you treat a very kind person, even if they are horrible.

Don't give in to your emotions. Try to let it go and continue to be polite. Don't interrupt, no matter how badly you want to; listen until they are done speaking. Take notes when you can to keep track of what they said.

Try not to raise your voice or overpower them; let them talk. If you speak at the same time, stop as soon as you recognize it, apologize, and let them go first.

When possible, ask the customer to hold; this will give you and the customer time to calm down.

If they get upset, listen and let them vent. It may be hard to hear, but it will let them calm down. Being extra polite in this situation takes it from a good experience to a great experience.

Even Though You Are Frustrated, Let It Go

Do not show frustration towards the customer; always be patient and give them enough time to ask questions, gather information, and understand your message. Do not argue with customers or talk over the top of them. It makes the situation a lot more tense.

Your goal is to make them feel respected and heard. You may not be able to do precisely what the customer asks, but if you are polite and treat them with respect, you will give them the best experience possible, and your customers will appreciate that, even though they might not say it.

Take Responsibility For Any Mistakes You Have Made

Always apologize, especially if you make a mistake. Be specific when you apologize. For example: "After researching more, I discovered I gave you some incorrect information; I'm sorry. Here is the correct information."

Humor and Possibly Offensive Language

Don't use any offensive language. Respect everyone from any culture.

Use humor carefully and only positive humor. You never know how someone is going to react to a joke.

If you are unsure if it would be appropriate, or if they may not understand, don't use it; find a different way to connect with them.

Finances and Other Sensitive Subjects

People get very uncomfortable talking about their finances and react by being upset. As a customer service provider, that means you are the one who takes the brunt of that anger. Understanding this about your customers makes it easier to continue to be polite when they are not being polite to you.

Listen to your customer explain their situation. If they start to get agitated, continue to listen. The most polite thing you can do is listen to what they say. Hear them out. In most cases, the customer calms down because they feel heard.

When you reply, avoid being argumentative. Also, be aware of your tone; make sure you sound polite and calm. Don't interrupt; this will quickly create an argument.

Show respect for their situation and feelings. Money is a very touchy subject and makes a lot of people uncomfortable. It will help decrease tension and negativity and show the customer that you respect them and their situation.

Notes:

Be Polite

Communicate Clearly

I have to repeat myself all the time.

When I first started, I would explain something to a customer, and they struggled to understand what I was saying, so I would have to repeat it. When listening to the call again with my coach, I could barely understand what I was saying. I was talking very fast and went back and forth several times. I started practicing and took the time to ask myself how I should explain it. I was able to shorten the explanation and stay on track to make it easier to understand.

"We can't do that." "You can, that's great."

A customer was calling to request a refund for a product that was delivered late. Per our policy, we cannot issue a refund for late deliveries. So I said, "We can't do that." They immediately responded, "You can, that's great!" I repeated, "We can't do that." They said, "Thank you," and ended the call. It was over so quickly that I didn't have another chance to explain that we were not able to issue a refund.

I have since learned to say, "No, we cannot do that." or "I am sorry, we cannot issue a refund," to make sure they understand me.

Don't say three 9's.

I had a call where I had to give the customer a confirmation code. They are about 12 digits long, so I sometimes look for shortcuts. This code had three 9s in a row, 999, so I thought I would save time by saying "three 9s". When the customer repeated the code back to me, they said "3 9" instead of "9 9 9". This meant their code was two digits short. I repeated the code and tried to emphasize "three 9s". They said, "That's the code I have! Why did you say it was wrong?" I clarified that the code was "9 9 9" and they got it. It took an extra five minutes to undo the confusion I caused, and the customer was very frustrated with me.

I still don't understand.

While working for a credit card company, I interacted with a customer who simply did not understand what I was trying to explain. I had already repeated myself two times, and I was starting to get frustrated because I did not know how else to say it. At this point in the conversation, the customer asked me another question, and I decided to place them on hold while I looked it up for them.

While I had them on hold, I took a few deep breaths to calm myself down and gather my thoughts. Within a few moments, I had an idea about how to explain it better. In my notepad, I made an outline of the process and the steps I was trying to explain. I broke it down to one step at a time. When I returned to my customer, I answered the question they had asked me, then mentioned I may have a better way to explain the process and asked if I could try again. They agreed.

I started slow, giving them only the first step. Then, I waited to give the customer some time to process what I said. After a moment, they said, "Okay, that makes sense." So, I moved on to the second step and then waited. This time, they said, "I have a question about that." I took the time to answer their question and ensure they understood everything related to the second step in the process before we moved on to step three. I followed this process until we got through all the steps.

At the end of our conversation, the customer thanked me several times for explaining it to them. They also stated that this was the third time they had called to get help with this same problem, and they got so frustrated the first two times that they just hung up.

Hearing that I helped the customer honestly made my day. I felt so bad they went through all of that, and it only took me a few minutes to adapt my explanation to help them understand. That is when I realized that communicating is not just about saying the message but how you present it and ensuring the customer understands it. I have been explaining complicated situations this way ever since.

What Is "Communicate Clearly"?

Every time you speak, it should be easy to understand. Only use words the customer will understand; do not use difficult words, technical phrases, internal phrases, or jargon.

Match the customer's pace. If they are going slow, you should slow down as well. Speak slowly and give them more time to understand your message. If they speak fast, try to go fast, but not so quickly they don't understand.

Clear your throat, drink water, catch your breath, etc., before you start talking. If your message is uninterrupted, it will be easier to comprehend.

Text Communication Must Be Clear

Clear communication is even more critical when communicating through written text. These conversations are less free-flowing and slower than voice conversations. It takes longer to explain your message, and it is easy for a customer to misunderstand your tone or phrasing and become offended or upset. If you get it wrong, you may not get another chance to correct yourself. Always read through the message before sending it to the customer.

Why It's Important

When customers can understand you clearly, you will develop trust, and they will feel comfortable asking more questions. They will also feel satisfied with your help and become repeat customers, who will also refer their friends and family.

If the customer cannot understand you, they will be confused, frustrated, and possibly even angry. The interaction can escalate and become increasingly difficult.

You don't want to repeat yourself; it can create an uncomfortable experience, waste the customer's time, and create confusion.

If the customer does not understand the message, they will have to contact us again for the same issue, which wastes their time. They may even end their business with us. The customer may not need to understand how we will solve their problem, but they must know what to expect during the process. Knowing what to expect will prevent further issues and mistakes.

> **Hard Definition:**
>
> We must always communicate as clearly as possible and ensure the customer has understood us.
>
> Ask questions to ensure they have understood you and always be willing to re-explain.

How To "Communicate Clearly"

Before speaking or typing, think about the message you must communicate, make it as clear as possible, and ensure the customer has understood it.

What you say and when you say it is crucial. Explain complicated processes in small, easy-to-understand parts and explain them in the correct order so the customer can follow. Make sure they understand before you move on to the next piece.

> I am pretty bad at telling stories; I get ahead of myself and start talking about the punch line before I am finished. When the story is over, no one is laughing. Then I realized I got so excited about the ending that I left out the key details that make it funny. When I repeat it again, with the necessary details, it's funny because now it makes sense.

Try to understand the customer's needs and adapt to them. You can go a bit slower to give them enough time to understand or go faster because they are in a hurry. Matching the customers' pace will make them feel more comfortable and show that we care about them.

In-Person (Face-To-Face) and Video Calls

When you provide service in person, and a customer asks you a question, ensure you are close enough for them to hear your response. If not, move closer before trying to respond. Try to make eye contact; it will show you are paying attention and want to hear what they say.

Be aware of your facial expressions. Do you look happy or sad? It's hard for a customer to approach you if you look angry and do not want to help.

Make sure you are smiling or have a friendly look on your face. Do not glare or make faces as a response to what they say. Remain polite and professional.

Be aware of the customer's comfort level and avoid crossing personal boundaries. Avoid touching or making contact. Most people do not like to be touched by people they do not know.

Email or Text

Clear communication is crucial when communicating by email or text. These messages are not live; you don't have the opportunity to re-explain immediately. If the customer does not reply, you will never have the chance to explain again. Ensure you provide all the information the customer may need when you reply.

Keep your response as short as possible, but ensure you convey the entire message.

It's Every Customer's First Time

As a provider, you have explained the process hundreds, possibly thousands, of times before, but this is the customer's first time. Remember that, be patient, and go at their speed. You can also suggest they write it down. If you do, make sure you give them time to do so.

Complicated Processes

For complicated explanations, slow down, even if they are in a hurry. Slow is smooth, and smooth is fast. Smooth is easier to understand. Making even little mistakes will take longer because you will have to re-explain it.

It is okay to make mistakes. When you realize you have, apologize, go back, and explain it correctly. You may need to start over entirely.

During long explanations, pause to give them time to understand and ask questions. Correctly timing your responses will make it much easier for them to understand. When communicating over email or text, split things into paragraphs for easier understanding. Every new topic, subject, or question should be the start of a new paragraph.

Do not bury an important message or question inside a paragraph, especially if the customer needs to take action. You should begin a new paragraph and make the message or action the focus of that paragraph.

Ask A Question, Wait For A Answer

Don't ask a question and not wait for the answer. You will interrupt the customer when they try to answer.

Never ask rhetorical questions, either. They are confusing, can be distracting, and usually create more negativity,

Try Not To Interrupt

Wait for the customer to finish explaining before you respond, even though you know the answer. It may be hard for them to understand your response if you talk at the same time. Hear them out and then respond.

If you speak at the same time, apologize and let them speak first.

Pause for 1-2 seconds before you respond to ensure they are finished. If they have more to say, they will keep going. When they finish, repeat the problem back to them to confirm you understand.

When you wait until your customer is finished speaking to respond, you show them respect and want to hear what they have to say. Cutting them off before they are finished shows you don't care and you think what you have to say is more important. Customers will not come back if that is how they are treated.

Let Customers Interrupt You

Customers often interrupt you, talk over you, and ignore what you say. It is easy to get frustrated and give in to the urge to talk over them to make your point finally. Do not do it. It is not worth it.

Every time I gave in to this urge, it did not go well. The customer became very upset, they argued even more, and eventually, the call escalated. They always calm down when I let them interrupt me and get everything out, and the interaction goes much smoother.

Use the "Be Polite" best practice, be patient, and wait for your chance to finish.

Spelling And Numbers

Use phonetic spelling all the time; don't try to spell over the phone without it. You can use the NATO or military alphabet or popular names or words. Whatever you feel comfortable with, use the same alphabet every time so you don't get confused.

When saying numbers like 888-512-1132, never say "three 8s" or "two 1s." Instead, say "eight, eight, eight" and "one, one." It is too confusing, and you will have to repeat it.

When repeating the number to the customer, the rep said, "Is that one one? Two ones?" The customer thought she said "one one two one" and got upset at her for not listening.

In this situation, it would be better to say, "Was that one one?" and then wait. Even saying, "Was that two ones?" can be confusing; it will sound like "two ones".

Intense Interactions

Take a breath or pause before you respond. This will allow you to calm down and think before you speak.

Slow your pace down; it can be very effective in heated and uncomfortable situations. Rushing makes your heart beat faster, which makes the interaction more intense for you and your customers. Slowing down will slow your heart rate and allow you to control the pace, helping you keep things as calm as possible.

Going too slow can make the customer feel as if you are insulting their intelligence. Pay attention to their verbal cues. If the tension has lessened, speed up as long as it won't create tension again.

Don't Use Sarcasm

Avoid speaking in a way that will upset them more. When a customer is rude and sarcastic, it is easy to want to say things that will annoy them because they are doing it to you. Do not give in to this urge. This is one of the most essential skills you need if you want to be successful.

Giving Bad News

Be completely honest with a customer about the situation. Don't beat around the bush; be clear and confident. Giving bad news is never fun, but honesty and transparency will help them accept it. Keep it simple. Here are some examples:

"I'm afraid I have some bad news. The shipment was delayed in transit and will arrive on Monday. "

"I want to be sure you understand what will happen. If we do not receive the required information by this day, your account will be closed".

"I would like to go over the terms again because I don't want you to be surprised or have something unexpected happen."

"Please be aware that if the payment is not received by this day, you will be billed a past-due fee."

"I want to be clear and upfront with you. A late fee will be applied if the payment is received after the cutoff on the due date."

Never hide the bad news or leave information out to sugar-coat it. Hearing the truth is a much better experience for the customer than waking up in the morning to a $40 past-due fee, etc. The customer will call back furious, saying no one ever told them that would happen.

No one wants to be the provider that has to take that call.

Notes:

Communicate Clearly

Listen to Understand

"I work for your credit card company."

While working for a credit card company, a customer kept saying, "I'm calling to pay my T-Mobile bill." At first, I was confused; why would you call your credit card company to pay your T-Mobile bill? I kept listening, and eventually, I realized that they had recently used their credit card to pay their T-Mobile bill and were calling to pay off that transaction.

This interaction taught me a lot about how customers sometimes say things differently than we are used to. It didn't make sense to me, but it made perfect sense to the customer.

"I need you to cancel my order so I can pick it up. "

When I first started working for an online pharmacy, I had a customer who called in and said, "I need you to cancel my order so I can pick it up."

It sounded odd to me. I thought to myself, "If I cancel your order, you won't be able to pick it up because you canceled it." So, I started asking some questions and finally clued into what they meant.

The customer wanted to cancel the order they placed with our pharmacy so they could pick it up at the local pharmacy instead. In this industry, the phrase "I want to cancel my order so I can pick it up" is very common. I just wasn't used to it yet.

Why was it shipped separately?!

I once had a customer who kept asking, "Why was it shipped separately?" over and over. I looked up the tracking number, and there was only one package. He assured me there were two packages being shipped.

I researched it, and there was only one package. I explained that I only found one package, not two. He said, "No, there are two packages coming. There should only be one. Why was it shipped separately?" I said, "I am not sure, but I will try to find out."

I did more research, asked my manager, and contacted other departments, but I still could not explain why it was in two packages. I could only find one. By this time, I had spent almost 30 minutes trying to find an answer.

I went back and explained I could not find any reason why it would have been shipped in two packages. He then gave me the second tracking number for the second package. I tracked the package, and it was from the same company and shipped at the same time. I immediately realized what was going on.

Almost right on cue, he said, "It's not your fault; it was theirs. They keep sending it in two packages, even though there is no reason it can't be in one package."

He continued to tell me this was an ongoing issue with the company he purchased from. He was calling to ensure there was no reason we would have required them to ship it in separate packages.

When he kept asking, "Why was it shipped separately?" I wasn't really thinking, and I should have picked up on the fact that the company who shipped it put it in two packages, not us. He needed to call the company he purchased the items from to find out why.

What Is "Listen to Understand"?

When listening to the customer, try to understand what they are trying to say. What do they really need help with? In most cases, the customer only knows what happened to them; they don't know what they need help with. They have a confusing story to explain what happened, and they may use the wrong words or say things incorrectly as they explain them.

You know more than they do; you are the expert. You must listen to and interpret what they say and then determine their needs. This is an essential part of providing a great experience.

Look beyond their words to the meaning of what they are saying. Ask questions if you don't understand and continue to ask until you understand.

Why It's Important

If you understand what they are trying to communicate, you can solve all of their issues, both the ones they actively mention and the ones they may not mention. You will prevent future issues and provide complete satisfaction in one interaction.

More satisfied customers will mean better reviews and scores for you. Customers will feel respected and understood because you know what they need. This will lead to happy customers, repeat business, and referrals.

You will understand the customer's needs faster. No time needs to be wasted re-explaining the details.

If you don't understand what they are really trying to say, you may miss a problem or their real concern. If they don't get the help they need, they will have to contact you again, and they will be annoyed and frustrated.

Solving their real or most important problems will show your commitment to providing great experiences. This will lead to happy customers, repeat business, and referrals.

Your customers will feel appreciated and respected; they will know you care and will help them. This builds trust, one of the most important things for keeping and turning customers into repeat customers.

> **Hard Definition:**
>
> We must do everything possible to understand what our customers are attempting to say and what outcome they expect.
>
> We are the experts, and we must be able to interpret what our customers are trying to communicate.

How To "Listen to Understand"

Always listen to everything they have to say. Write down the important details so you can remember them later. Then, ask questions to help you understand their problem.

Be patient. Wait until they finish. Even if you already know the answer, hear them out. They may have other important information to add, and it is polite.

Pay attention to what they are saying. Don't get distracted or try to multitask. If in person, make eye contact as much as possible and focus on them.

Don't cut the customer off. If they struggle to explain their point, ask them a clarifying question to help you understand. This may show them a path and then be their guide.

Set aside your own judgments and try to see things from their point of view. Listen beyond all of their emotions to find the real problem.

Asking Questions Is Just As Important As Listening

Ask questions. The most important part of understanding is asking questions. If you are unsure, ask clarifying questions until you understand. Never assume or jump to a conclusion. You don't have to. You will have time to find out exactly what they mean.

Ask open-ended questions, such as questions that can't be answered with just a yes or no answer.

Repeat Back What You Understand

Once you feel you understand, tell them what you understand and give them a chance to correct you if you don't understand.

If they do correct you, take it graciously. You can say, "Thank you for clarifying. Now I understand what you meant."

Pay Attention to Recurring Words Or Phrases

Listen for patterns and words or phrases that they repeat. These are a clue to an underlying issue they may be having. Listen for keywords or phrases like:

- I am worried.
- This doesn't feel right.
- What should I do?
- I don't know how this works.
- This is concerning.
- This is so confusing.
- I am scared this will happen again.
- I've never had to do this before.

These will help guide you to their problems and find their real concerns.

Help Them Find The Product They Want

When customers are looking for a product but don't know the name, they will try to describe the item, and it can be challenging to determine what they are looking for. Listen for things you recognize and consider what they could be looking for. You have to try to understand what they are trying to say beyond the actual words they are saying.

Ask questions about the product. What does it look like? What does it do, or what is it used for? Do they have a picture? Ask a co-worker if they know where it is.

They Talk About The Side Effects, Not The Cause

Are they complaining about the side effects of the issue? Are they using the wrong words or phrases? But saying something different, like "You guys have the worst shipping system" or "What are you going to do to make it up to me or compensate me for my time?"

They may say, "I have never had to do this before", instead of asking why it is different this time.

They Will Use The Wrong Words, Names, Phrases

When customers call to report fraud or dispute a charge on their debit or credit card, they are unaware of how the card works and will not use the correct terminology. Most customers will say a charge is fraudulent, and then later in the conversation, you will find out they were just charged more than they expected. They reported it as a fraudulent charge because, in their mind, that is fraudulent.

Try to help them understand the correct process and explain the terminology. Explain the difference between fraud and a dispute.

In this case, the correct process is to file a dispute. Reporting the charge as fraud will create more problems for the customer and delay the outcome by at least 30 days.

To ensure you do it correctly, listen to why they are reporting fraud or disputing the charge, ask questions until you are sure which it is, and then explain the process so they know what to expect.

What About Emails, Chats, or Text Messages?

When working on emails and chats, reading is the same as listening. Look for patterns, keywords, or keyphrases like you would listen for them.

Reading the message as if speaking directly to the customer can be helpful. Text does not always convey the emotions the customer may be feeling. By "acting out" the message, you can apply tone and inflections to better understand it.

Try to understand what the customer is actually concerned with so you can respond to everything they have contacted you about.

Try This Example:

A customer called to report that she did not get her monthly statement, and then she started complaining about things she heard on the news about customer service.

She heard that people are being told to go to websites instead of getting help from a customer service agent. She mentioned again that she didn't get her statement until after the due date, then started talking about what she had heard on the news again. She mentioned she felt bad for elderly people being told to go to websites with pages and pages of information, and they don't know how to use websites.

What was this customer concerned about?

She mentioned not receiving her statement, but her main concern was that she wouldn't get help when she called to speak with customer service. She was worried she would be told to go to the website and solve the problem herself. She didn't want to do that. She wanted to speak with a representative and have the statement mailed to her.

How would you respond to this customer?

I said, "I understand your concern. Good customer service is important, and I want to let you know that you can call in to speak with an agent anytime. We are here to help. I would be happy to mail you a duplicate copy of your statement." Then I added, "We do have a few processes that need to be completed online. When that happens, please give us a call, and we can walk you through them step by step."

Her demeanor changed immediately. She let out a huge sigh and said she was relieved to hear that.

In this example, I heard what she was really worried about, which was being told to do it herself and not being able to speak with an agent, and I made sure to address it in my response. I also made sure to address what she said the problem was: she did not receive her statement.

Notes:

Be A Guide

Why are they not following my instructions?

When I started in customer service, I was often frustrated with customers who called to ask for help and then did not follow my instructions. It was so difficult having to repeat the instructions over and over and then have the customer get mad at you because it's not working.

It felt like they weren't listening on purpose, and it really made me mad. The instructions were simple and easy to follow and would solve their problem; I did not understand why they did not listen to the instructions that would solve their problem.

What am I doing wrong? Why don't they understand what I am telling them?

I was trying to explain to a customer how the dispute process works for their credit card, but they just did not understand. After I explained it twice, they asked for a supervisor. I was very frustrated because I knew I was telling them correctly. I transferred to the supervisor and continued to listen to the call.

I noticed that the supervisor said the same things I did to explain it, but they took a different approach. They told the customer the first step and then waited until the customer said, "Okay, I understand that." Then, they explained the second step and waited for the customer to respond. After the supervisor explained the third step, the customer jumped in and said, "Oh, okay, and then I will get the chance to respond or get a credit on my account."

It became obvious to me what I was doing wrong. I was explaining it correctly but not giving the customer enough time to understand.

"No offense, but I hope I don't speak to you again."

I remember walking a customer through updating their address and requesting a new card. He specifically said, "Show me how to do it so I can do it on my own." So I started telling him the steps, one by one. Soon, he started to recognize what the next steps were on his own. Since he was moving forward on his own, I only jumped in when he asked, "Okay, what's next?". I asked if he wanted to go through it again, so we did, and he walked through the steps again.

In the end, he was very appreciative and said, "I mean no offense, but I hope I don't speak to you again." He laughed and said, "Thanks again, bye."

What Is "Be A Guide"?

A guide will show you the way, not just tell you how. They will let you lead the adventure, but they will also answer any questions you have and offer tips along the way.

You should use this approach when helping customers, even for simple tasks. Show them the way; don't just tell them how. Allow them to lead, but guide them along the way.

This will empower them to solve their problems on their own and build confidence and trust in you, the products, services, and the company.

You don't have to be in control. Recognize where the customer is coming from and focus on explaining the solution. Walk the customer through the solution, but allow them to go at their own pace and complete the task independently.

Don't decide for the customer. Explain all the possible options and let them choose what is best. Then, guide them to the solution.

A good guide can show you exactly how to do it, point you toward the next step, and make you feel like you found the answer on your own.

If the customer does not want to do it themselves, do it for them. Always give them a chance to try it for themselves, but don't force it if they protest. If you can't do it for them and they continue to protest, tell them you understand and politely explain that you cannot do it for them, but you will guide them through it.

You do not have to be in control to be a guide. There is a difference.

Difference Between Guidance and Control

Guidance is about communication and patience with the common goal of solving the problem. Control is about getting your way regardless of the other person's needs or feelings.

You can control which option they select by only offering the one you prefer, or you can tell them all the options available and guide them through the pros and cons.

Guiding is letting the customer know it is okay to take their time and ask questions. Controlling is insisting that they do it your way and at your pace.

Guidance is polite. Control is rude.

Guidance is subtle and gentle. Control is harsh and overpowering.

Great experiences happen when customers feel empowered to solve problems and have a positive outlook. Guide your customers to the solution to empower them without making them feel stupid or rushed.

Why It's Important

If you guide your customers, they will feel respected. You are helping them solve their problem without "rubbing it in" that they don't know what to do. You are simply pointing them in the right direction so they can complete the task.

This will empower them to solve their problems independently and build confidence and trust in you, the products/services, and the company.

Customers are more likely to remember it when they "figure it out on their own" versus being told how to do it.

It's likely that the customer has already tried to solve this problem on their own and was unsuccessful. They may be feeling stupid, embarrassed, or frustrated. If you can guide them, they will feel like they figured it out on their own. They will feel more confident and empowered to stay self-sufficient.

The satisfaction of finding the correct answer is a strong feeling. People remember those feelings. If we can help our customers feel confident enough to do it on their own, they will continue to do business with us. A self-reliant customer becomes a repeat customer and spends more money when they visit.

Most people don't like to be told what to do, even when they are asking you how to do something. It makes them feel insecure, incapable, and embarrassed. Guiding someone rarely has that effect. Guiding allows the customer to feel confident and in control while still getting your help.

> ### Hard Definition:
> We must always educate and guide the customer through our processes.
>
> Never try to control their actions, and always give them a chance to become self-sufficient.

How To "Be a Guide"

Let go of your need to be in control of everything. Be patient. Learn to listen. Allow the customer to go at their pace and be willing to repeat the steps and the answers to questions they may ask again.

Let them know it is okay, "It's okay, I understand. I would be happy to show you."

A good guide knows what is coming next. We are familiar with the system and the processes, but the customer is not. Use our foresight to help them see where to go. Briefly explain what needs to be done, then guide them from step to step. Let them do the next step if they figure it out. If they don't figure it out on their own, show them.

Let the customer lead the conversation. They will let you know when they are ready to move on. Be prepared to show them the next step.

Great experiences happen when you work with the customer and find a solution to their problem. You want the experience to be as fluid and graceful as possible, so you need to flow with the customer, not against them.

Be aware of where your customer is coming from and their emotions. Here are some questions you can ask yourself to help you find out:

- How long have they been trying to solve this problem?
- Are they completely frustrated and ready to "lose it"?
- Are they embarrassed, so they apologize for wasting your time or thank you repeatedly?
- Are they worried because things are not going as planned?
- Are they first-time customers?
- How familiar are they with the system they are using?

Understanding where your customers are coming from will help you adapt your style to theirs. Some people need more patience and empathy; others may need to vent or share feedback. It's important to recognize what your customer needs and adjust.

Use the "Communicate Clearly" and "Listen to Understand" practices. Listen to your customers to find out what they need help with, where they are coming from, and their emotions. Then, ask questions to help you gather more information. Pay attention to their feelings as you go. Try to make the customer feel more comfortable by assuring them you will do everything possible to help them. Purposely slow down. Going slower will help you control your emotions and help the customer understand.

Before you start, briefly explain or break down the process steps so the customer knows what they are about to experience. Sometimes, customers don't have all the necessary information they need with them, or maybe they don't have enough time to complete the entire process. In these situations, a good guide would tell the customer what they will need and approximately how long it will take so the customer can be prepared next time.

Go through each step one by one. Explain what you are doing and allow the customer to ask questions. Allow the conversation to go at their pace; don't rush them. Match the customer's flow. As you explain, give them one piece of information at a time, and make sure they understand it before you move on. Ask questions to find out where they are in the process. Guide them toward where to go next.

Explain All The Options

When there are multiple solutions or choices, give them all the possible options and the pros and cons of each choice. Don't tell them what to do; instead, encourage them to choose what is best for them.

Tell them how to avoid this problem in the future. You know more, so you should offer to help, even if the customer does not ask. You can also suggest things they may need to be aware of or have changed recently.

Spend time practicing guiding the customer through the complicated tasks. The more you practice, the better you will be.

Website Walkthroughs

Most companies have a website or app, and you will have to show your customers how to use it. Here is an example of how to guide them through it.

> "You can change that in your account settings. I can show you how to do that.
>
> Go to www.website.com and log in. Then, you will be asked to complete a text verification step.
>
> Now, you should see a menu in the upper right corner; click on Settings, then Update Personal Info."

Be specific about where things are located, such as in the upper right corner, the third option in the list, or to the left of the shopping cart.

Complicated Processes

When explaining a complicated process or policy, break it down into smaller steps and ensure the customer understands each step before moving on.

For example, "First, we need to make sure you meet all of the qualifications. If so, we will need to contact your bank to verify the payment. The process usually takes about 25 minutes." or "We are going to verify your email, then I will give you an account recovery token. After that, you will be able to reset your password."

Notes:

Be A Guide

Same Way Every Time

Did I forget to...

I do not like the feeling I get when I realize I forgot to tell the customer something, and now the call is over. I always feel so bad because I intended to tell them; I just forgot, but now they may have a bad experience because of it. Usually, if I forget something, it is a small detail that I like to share to help make things easier for the customer next time.

One time, I forgot to mention that their account would be on hold while we made the changes they requested.

This meant the customer could only place orders once the hold was removed. This customer had mentioned that they needed to place more orders soon, and I knew they would be alarmed when they logged into their account and saw that it was on hold.

I spoke to my supervisor and got permission to call the customer back and tell them about the hold. After that, I created a checklist for this process so I would always remember.

Stop these escalated calls

We had a complicated policy change that our reps struggled to explain. Customers were confused and upset. Over 60% of the calls were escalated to supervisors. Halfway through the first week, my team became frustrated and struggled to keep taking calls.

After talking to a few of my team members, I realized what the problem was. They needed a clear definition of how to explain the changes and respond to angry customers. The other team leaders and I met that night to listen to the calls and find a better way.

It took about 3 hours and a lot of discussing (sometimes arguing), but we devised a very simple and clear script and explained all the changes in a way everyone understood. We also created a list of frequently asked questions and better answers for the questions.

The next day, each team leader worked with groups of reps until we taught them the scripts. The reps were very happy to finally understand the changes and have some tools to deal with these hard calls. Everyone was finally on the same page. The calls started going great, and only 20% of them were escalated.

What Is "Same Way Every Time"?

Every customer deserves the same great experience. How can you achieve that when each interaction is different? Simple: find the best way to do it and do it that way for every customer every time. Each interaction can still be different, but each time you perform a task or complete a process, do it the same way every time.

Once you find the best way to complete a task, document the steps somewhere you can access them during your interactions. Every time you perform that task, follow your directions to ensure you get the same outcome. Don't skip any steps; do them in order and follow all the instructions.

Why It's Important

Doing it the same every time reduces errors, prevents omissions, and achieves the same outcome each time. Every time customers interact with you, they will receive all the information they need. This will build trust and make your job easier.

You won't lose your place if you get distracted, interrupted, or confused, or the customer does. You will know what comes next and be able to pick up where you left off.

You will not be worried that you forgot something or skipped a step.

> *If you forget to give a customer the return authorization number, they will have to call us back to get the number and again when we receive the item. It seems simple, but it is easy to forget because they are always in a hurry, and the situation is stressful. I hate taking calls when they do not get the number.*

You can multitask more efficiently and confidently. Doing the same thing every time makes your job easier. Each task becomes a habit and builds muscle memory. Your day will go better and become more consistent. You will feel less stressed and hectic, and you will feel more in control.

It will lower the chance of errors or breaches and ensure better compliance with the rules and regulations.

When you do it with the right mindset, your days will become consistent instead of mundane. The goal is to provide every customer with the same excellent service. With that goal in mind, you will feel proud of your work and not bored.

You will also have better stats, which can lead to bonuses and promotions. Your customer satisfaction ratings (NPS, CSAT, etc.) and quality assurance scores will be higher and more consistent.

> **Hard Definition:**
>
> Once we find the best way to complete a task, we must document the steps and follow these directions every time we perform the task.

How To Do It The "Same Way Every Time"

Find the best way to perform each task or process, document the steps, and follow those instructions every time.

Start using your "How-To" steps to ensure you are always compliant. Follow any predefined guidelines. They have been developed over time to be efficient and effective. Usually, this will be the best way to do it; once we learn it, you should do it the same way every time.

This is even more important with a more complicated process. There will be lots of information to explain and many steps to follow. Break it into more manageable parts, make them as simple as possible, and use those parts in that order every time.

Finding The Best Way

Finding the best way will require experimentation. When you have performed a task many times, you become familiar with it. When you notice a confusing or awkward part, possibly a missing step, or a step that could be reordered, start experimenting with a new way to do it.

Try something different, and pay attention to the outcome. Only change one thing at a time; you may need to try it five to ten times to know if it will work.

Document the change you are making and record the outcomes each time you perform that task. This will help you decide whether to continue the change or return to the original. Sometimes, this can be a long process, but finding the best way is worth the wait.

Work With Your Team

Learn from each other. If you find something that works well with your customers, share it with your teammates. If it worked for you, it should work for them. Test out ways to say things with each other and use the best ones.

If you find a process that needs to be defined or improved, mention this to your coach or team leader. If you are maintaining your own "How To," be sure to add it here as well.

Treat Every Customer Like They Are A Good Customer

Treat every customer the same way. Every customer deserves your best experience. You feel better about yourself when you respect other people. Treat them like a good customer, and be happy to help them.

Use the same greeting at the beginning of every communication. Put in the same amount of effort for each customer. We understand this is not always easy when the customer is hard to work with.

Use the "Be Polite" and "Listen to Understand" practices to help you along the way.

Regulated Industries

The processes in regulated industries must be completed correctly to avoid regulation issues and fines and to protect customers from potential harm. These processes should be performed the same way every time to help ensure steps are not missed and mistakes are not made.

For example, in banking, there is a process to release the funds for a pending payment before it is posted to the account so the customer can use the money immediately. This process has a lot of pre-qualifications that you have to check to release the funds.

If you forget to check one qualifier or forget to tell the customer that it could take 10 - 30 mins, depending on their bank, you are getting their hopes up.

In most cases, they become furious because they depended on that money and now you are going back on what you said.

It is very uncomfortable to return to a customer and say, "Oh, I forgot to check this before we started, and you don't qualify. Sorry, I cannot do this for you." We got their hopes up, and now they are furious.

> I found that customers asked many more questions when I did not tell them the steps up front. This interrupted the flow of our conversation, which made them forget what we had already talked about, and we had to go over it again.
>
> It also created a more tense situation. Giving all the info upfront helped provide context to the process, resulting in a better understanding for the customer and, in most cases, fewer angry questions. I do it this way every time now.

How Do I Know It's The Best?

You need to track or quantify your results. Then, compare the results of each scenario and see which is better. Here are some questions to ask about each scenario to get you started:

- What did I say, and how did I say it?
- How did the customer react to what I said?
- Did they understand what I said, or were they confused?
- Did they ask more questions than usual or less?
- How do I feel about what happened? Do I feel positive or negative?
- Does it feel confrontational or argumentative?
- Do I regret anything I said or wish I had said it better?
- What is the overall result or outcome?

Add as many questions to your list as necessary to analyze the experience. The answers to these questions and your response from the customer will tell you if this was a good or bad change. Following this process will eventually lead you to the best way.

Notes:

Same Way Every Time

The Power of "Oh..."

Wait, what just happened?

I was having a very uncomfortable interaction with a customer. They yelled at me for a few minutes straight, and I was getting frustrated.

When I finally had a chance to respond, I said, "Oh," they paused, and I quickly said, "That sounds frustrating; I can look into that."

They stopped and said thank you. The dynamic of the conversation changed entirely. They were caught off guard, and I was able to turn things around.

I use it all the time now.

Oh no, I'm sorry that happened

Saying, "Oh no, I'm sorry that happened," is one of my favorites. Customers will call in furious about their packages not being received. They would always explain in detail what happened, usually very long explanations, and the longer they talk, the angrier they become.

When there was a pause in their explanation, I would say, "Oh no, I'm sorry that happened."

It's the perfect thing to say in this situation. They have been through something really frustrating and are looking for someone to understand them. In most cases, they start to calm down immediately and give me a chance to help them.

Oh...They're Not There

I first learned this trick while working in outbound collections for a credit card company. I was calling past-due customers and tried to get them to make a payment. When I first started, the most challenging part was getting the cardholder on the phone.

Whoever answered would pretend the cardholder was not home and tell me to call back later. My team leader paired me up with one of the top reps, and they taught me to respond with, "Oh... they're not there?"

The person on the other end will think this is a personal call and be more compliant. They usually say, "Maybe they are here; let me check," and then the cardholder will get on the phone.

It worked very well. It disrupts their current thought pattern and changes the call's dynamic.

What Is "The Power of Oh..."?

When an interaction is not going as expected, it becomes tense or gets off on a negative track, use an "Oh..." statement to disrupt the conversation without offending the customer.

Say "Oh" and pause momentarily, then follow it with a statement that fits the situation.

For example, "Oh no... that should not have happened. Let me get that fixed for you," or "Oh wow... I have never heard that before. I would be happy to look at that for you."

It has the power to disrupt the conversation but in a good way. The customer does not expect you to say it, so it throws them off momentarily. Most will expect you to argue with them.

Now, you can focus on helping them. You have disrupted the conversation by surprising them with a statement of empathy and understanding instead of confrontation. This causes them to step back, and they will let you help.

Why It's Important

One of the hardest things about customer service is changing the flow of the conversation without offending the customer. Only a few things allow you to do this.

"Oh" statements are very effective and easy to use.

Your customers will be surprised at your concern. They will feel heard and understood. With one simple sentence, you confirm that you understand their problem, convey your intention to help and change the flow of the conversation.

> **Hard Definition:**
>
> We can use an "Oh..." statement to disrupt a negative conversation and change the flow without offending the customer.
>
> Say "Oh" and pause momentarily, then follow it up with a statement that fits the situation. For example, a statement that expresses empathy, concern, surprise, excitement, interest, etc.
>
> Each "Oh" statement must be genuine to be effective.

How To Apply "The Power of "Oh""

Say "Oh" and then pause before we respond. Say it as if we are surprised by what they are saying. Do it subtly. If it is too exaggerated, then it is obvious it is not genuine. Follow it up with a statement of empathy, action, or concern.

- "Oh ... that is odd."
- "Oh no, that is not good."
- "Oh wow, that is exciting."
- "Oh, okay, I'm sorry, that is not supposed to happen."
- "Oh no...I understand; I will see what options we have."
- "Oh no...I am sorry; I will check on your account."
- Oh no, that sounds terrible. Let me see how I can improve your day and fix this for you.
- "Oh wow...I am sorry; I will try to find out what happened."

You can use "Oh..." statements to express many different emotions, depending on what you say afterward and your tone. Use an "Oh..." statement that matches your customer's feelings.

- "Oh no..." shows concern.
- "Oh wow," shows surprise.
- "Oh, yes. That is one of my favorites," shows interest.
- "Oh. I forgot to tell you," shows excitement.
- "Oh no, I feel bad that happened," shows sadness.
- "Oh. That is frustrating," shows empathy.

When you use it, it has to be genuine. This is where you need to manage your tone. You cannot be monotone, arrogant, rude, or sarcastic; the customer will pick up on it, and things will escalate. It needs to be genuine if you want to stop the negativity and the bad flow.

Never Say

Never say, "Oh well" or "Oh, too bad"; that will do the opposite. It will make them upset and feel rejected.

Don't overuse it; it can lose its power. Don't say it at the beginning of every sentence. Only use it when you need it.

> *I have had some tense conversations with customers about past-due payments, closed accounts, and missing medications. I say, "Oh... I am sorry to hear that," and "Oh no, that is not supposed to happen" all the time. It always helps disrupt the conversation and allows me to calm things down and show them I will help.*

> *Customers are usually upset or frustrated when they have to return an item. Saying, "Oh... okay, I can help you with that," works very well for me.*

Use it when customers have had a frustrating or challenging experience. These calls are complicated because the stories can be difficult to listen to and sometimes hard to empathize with.

Next, you will learn the "Don't Judge" and "Avoid Negativity" best practices. When you apply these practices with "Be Polite", "Listen to Understand", and "The Power Of Oh," you will be able to provide a great experience, even in these difficult moments.

Notes:

The Power of "Oh..."

Don't Judge

"You got a late fee because you were late. Again."

It was my second year working at a credit card company. It felt like one of the longest days, and I had already taken 20 or so calls about past-due fees. I was talking to another customer who had a past-due fee, and they wanted it removed. They had been billed other past-due fees and wanted to know why they were billed a fee.

I was getting a little annoyed because they acted like it was unfair. In my head, I thought, "You got a late fee because you were late. Again."

Then, the call became confrontational, and I didn't like how I felt. I remember thinking, it does not matter what excuse you have; I can only do so much about the fee, and then I had an "ah-ha" moment.

I should do the same things to help this customer regardless of their reason, excuse, or sob story. I could not change what options I had available, even if they had a really good reason. So I told myself, "It doesn't matter why they got billed a fee; I should not judge them; just help them and let all that negativity go."

From that time on, my entire outlook changed; for every call I took, I tried very hard not to judge them. I just let it go and helped in any way I could.

What is her problem?

I was listening to an agent on my team take a call live. The call was not going well, and I could tell the agent was very uncomfortable and offended by what the customer said, even though the statements were not directed at her. After the call, the agent left their desk and went to the break room.

I waited for them to return and asked if they were okay. They were still upset, so I asked if we could talk about that call, not because they were in trouble but because they were really upset, and I wanted to help them. We went to a private room and started talking about it.

She said that she felt judged by that customer, which offended her. I told her I recognized this too, and as politely as possible, I told her it sounded like she (the agent) was being judgemental too. She seemed annoyed at the customer's excuse. She said, "I was annoyed. I hate it when customers think they can ignore our warnings about the cut-off time and then call in upset their package did not make it on time."

I let her know that bothered me, too, but it seemed the customer was upset with the company, not her. I told her that when we judge people, even a little bit, we will start to feel like they are judging us, too, even if they are not. We start worrying about what they will judge us for and instinctively become defensive and confrontational.

She quickly recognized what I pointed out and said, "You're right. They weren't upset or judging me; they were mad at the policy. Next time, I won't be so 'sassy' and judgemental."

Why are my CSAT stores negative? I am trying to be nice.

One of my representatives came to me and said they seemed to be getting negative customer satisfaction (CSAT) scores more often. They had been working hard to provide good service and were not sure why this kept happening. We listened to those calls and compared them to their calls with positive scores. After listening to the calls, I asked them, "What did you hear that was different between the types of calls?"

I could tell they were embarrassed at first because they recognized the difference in their tone, demeanor, and even how they talked to the customer. I asked them, "Why did your demeanor change on this call?" They responded, "I get annoyed with customers when they complain that they got billed a late fee, and then they treat me like crap when I can't waive it. I wanted to say, "You're late; of course, you got billed a fee. It's due on the same day every month. Maybe you should write that down."

I kindly pointed out that thinking like that and having that attitude meant they were judging the customer. In their head, they were calling the customer stupid and continued thinking that way for the remainder of the call. Even though they did not say it to the customer, their tone and responses made it obvious.

From there, we worked on finding ways for them not to judge the customers, even when they were annoying. I told them it technically did not matter why they got the late fee, and we started talking about how to handle it when the customer has a late fee because that is where they were struggling; then, we moved on to getting better at it overall.

After a few days, we had a follow-up conversation about how things were going. They said they started to notice that they didn't feel so annoyed with those calls, and it was getting easier to do it. I could tell their outlook had changed; they were happier to help customers and offered to teach their neighbors.

After a few weeks, I pulled their CSAT scores, and we noticed that they were back to getting positive scores, and their average had gone up by 22%. I told them how proud I was of them and pointed out that this small change greatly benefited them and our customers.

What Is "Don't Judge?"

Never judge a customer for any reason, especially when they are dealing with a problem. It doesn't matter what happened or why; the customer needs your help to find the solution. Never put your biases or emotions on the customer.

Judgment comes in many forms, and it can be very simple or deeply complex. Many thoughts and statements may not seem like judgment, but they are and will be felt by customers, no matter how small.

To provide the best experience, it must be free of judgment. Customers need to feel safe and respected while interacting with you. See every customer as an equal and help them all the same.

This practice is one of the hardest to perform but also provides the most benefit. Mastering it requires a lot of self-control and honesty.

Why It's Important

Judgment creates negativity, anger, and hatred. It puts you in a bad mood, ruins your day, and affects your coworkers. Your customers can hear it when you judge them. You will feel it when you judge them. It will come out in your tone and facial expressions, no matter how good your "acting" is.

When you focus on helping customers, you will feel better throughout the day. You will not carry those negative feelings around all day and will not take them home at the end of the day.

When you judge others, you feel like they are judging you, too, and you start to think the customer is going to criticize you or might make fun of you if you make a mistake. This makes you defensive. Your customers will feel that judgment, no matter how small. They will become defensive and confrontational and make the interaction very difficult.

If you don't judge your customers, they will feel comfortable telling you what happened and why; this will help you find the right solution.

When you judge consistently, you train your brain to find the bad in things. This will lead you to find something bad about every customer in every interaction. It can increase stress, fatigue, anxiety, and depression. You don't need to put yourself through that.

You will have a better attitude and mood, your coworkers will appreciate it, and customers will feel more comfortable interacting with you. It can help you let go of any negativity from the interaction; you will not be tied to it in any way.

> **Hard Definition:**
>
> We must never judge the customer for any reason. It does not matter what happened or why; we only need to resolve their issue.
>
> When you catch yourself judging a customer, stop immediately and let it go.

How To Apply "Don't Judge"

Focus on solving the problem rather than what caused the problem. Sometimes, the customer is the cause of their problems. It doesn't matter if they are; don't focus on who is to blame. Instead, focus on discovering what is wrong and striving to solve it.

To solve the problem, you may need to know how it happened to show the customer how to avoid it in the future. This can be a crucial step in finding the correct solution. If the customer did create their problem, do not judge them for doing so.

We are all people, and we make mistakes and do dumb things from time to time. Don't use this to judge or say something negative about your customers. Instead, focus on providing the best experience you can and solving their problems.

No Blame Zone

Use a blame-free approach. Do not blame the customer for what happened, even if it is their fault. Work to solve their issue.

Don't mute your phone or put the customer on hold and then say something negative about them. Don't even think about the negative things. Just start helping the customer. Fix their problem, and move on.

Even if they do it many times, for example, when you walk them through how to do something online, they click on everything except what you tell them to click on. Just be patient and keep trying to help. Take deep breaths to keep yourself calm. Don't say negative things about the customer, and don't say them to your coworkers, either.

It takes practice and discipline, but not judging your customers becomes second nature with time.

Be Careful What You Think

You cannot think or say things like:

> "I have told them millions of times, what an idiot."
> "Just do what I say."
> "That is not what I said to click on."
> "Oh my god, really, did you do that?"
> "Oh my god, you are so stupid"
> "I can't believe you did that".
> "Why do you keep doing that?!"

They are very judgemental, and you will treat the customer differently because you thought of them. I feel bad even saying them now, but I must mention them so everyone understands what I mean.

If you would never say it to a customer's face or in front of your boss, don't think it or say it behind their back. These comments are unnecessary; they only create anger and negativity, and you create it within yourself.

Take A Break, Get It Out

If you judge customers and can't stop or let it go, you may need to take a break or participate in a "Bitch Session". See the "Bitch Session" best practice to learn more.

Seek Facts, Never Assume

To avoid judging, seek out facts instead of making assumptions. Ask questions to find out what happened, not who caused it. Ask questions to determine the customer's desired outcome and help them get that result.

You need to deal with your feelings. If you feel nervous, insecure, or upset, you may judge others superficially to make yourself feel better. This does not work. You are not building yourself up; you are just tearing someone else down. This breeds feelings of negativity. You will feel it, and so will your customers.

Customers Are People Too

Treat them as a real person, the same as us. We all need help from time to time and ask seemingly stupid questions at times. When you are close to a problem, you may need help seeing the entire picture and often miss the obvious.

There Are No Stupid Questions

There is no such thing as a stupid question. It's just a question that the customer needs the answer to, so give it to them. It doesn't matter why they need it; they just do.

Be empathetic and forgiving. Use your core skills and other practices to express that you understand their feelings. Do not judge them based on their feelings or why they are having the problem. Forgive them for being upset or making a rude comment. Just focus on the solution.

No matter the industry, every company I have worked for has these types of questions. I am sure you can think of a few that you answer daily. It does not matter what the question is; the customer needs an answer. Answer without judgment to provide the best experience possible.

"When Is The 3:00 pm Parade?"

Famously, the Disney Institute teaches in its customer service training that the question, "When is the 3:00 pm parade?" is not stupid. How would you answer that question? It's an easy question to answer, but how do you avoid offending or making them feel stupid?

A great response would be: "Oh, that is my favorite one; you don't want to miss it. It's at 3:00 pm on Main St."

This way, you are not focusing on the fact that they said 3:00 pm in their question or making them feel stupid; you are simply answering their question and giving them more details.

Difficult Or Awkward Situations

When the coronavirus shutdown happened, we worked for a credit card company, and some customers struggled to make payments. They would call and ask what could be done because they could not pay. We felt terrible for their situation and happily helped them.

We also had some customers call in to make a payment, then stop and say, "Oh, wait. What are you guys doing for the Coronavirus?" Then, they would change their story and claim they could not make their payment.

I found that the agents were having a more difficult time not judging these customers than the ones who were having a hard time because it was clear these customers were not being honest.

It is not your job to catch customers in a lie. Unless your employer says explicitly you need to call out your customers, you don't need to do that.

A customer called on Tuesday, 12/26, and said they had mailed a check on Friday, 22 December, and wanted to know why it had yet to arrive. The customer should have considered that it was the weekend, not to mention the Christmas holiday. USPS is typically closed on Sundays and 12/25.

It seemed obvious to me that if you mail something on Friday, 12/22, it will not be delivered anytime soon. Probably two weeks at the earliest. But this customer did not get it.

In the end, I was able to waive their past-due fee. It honestly did not matter why they were late. All I did was waste my time and create negativity for myself by judging them.

Notes:

Don't Judge

Avoid Negativity

I hated the way I felt at the end of the day.

I started to notice that I hated how I felt at the end of the day. Some of the people I worked with were always negative about everything, like customers, work policies, coworkers, etc. So, I started avoiding conversations with them. After a while, I noticed that now, when I get off work, I feel so much better. It felt like an enormous weight had been lifted.

Every little piece of negativity stuck with me.

I was having a terrible day at work. When my coach noticed, they pulled me aside and asked me what was happening. I said, "I am not sure. It just feels like everything is pulling me down today."

They told me they noticed I had been complaining about customers with my neighbors and mentioned how that could affect my feelings. It was obvious when I thought about it, but I never considered it. So, I stopped participating in those conversations and even moved my seat to be around other agents. My interactions with customers improved, I did not feel dragged down, and my CSAT score went up.

The customers' negativity is not my own.

When a customer is dealing with a bad situation, I always try to show empathy and understand where they are coming from, but by the end of the day, I feel so negative and angry. On the way home, I found myself being rude and impatient with the people working at the drive-thru or grocery store.

When I realized it, I felt self-conscious because these people were doing a similar job to mine, but it was harder, and I was one of their rude, negative customers for the day. I did not like this.

I had to learn that the customer's negativity is not mine, and I can show empathy without taking the burden upon myself. I don't have to feel the same way as them. I need to recognize how they feel, try to solve the problem, and then let it go.

What Is "Avoid Negativity"?

Providing good customer experiences is a difficult job. People can be hard to work with, argumentative, and rude. This tends to weigh on us, and we can develop a negative attitude. Negativity is a heavy burden that spreads like wildfire, so we must do our best to avoid it.

Stop thinking or saying negative things, and avoid reacting to customers' comments and remarks.

Being negative makes you feel terrible about yourself, your job, and your customers. It will affect your mood and attitude, and it can affect your coworkers. It will bring you down. The customers you interact with can tell, and this will lead to bad experiences.

Think of a negative comment like a 5-pound weight; every time you say something negative, you pick up a weight. Throughout the day, you pick up another weight whenever you say or hear something negative. You carry that weight around with you everywhere. You take it into your next interaction and, most likely, for the rest of the day. If you pick up a negative comment from every customer, how much weight will you carry throughout the day? What would your total be at the end of the day?

Not many people can carry this weight; I know I can't. This practice is about avoiding this negativity so you don't have to.

> *Negativity can make you sad, angry, annoyed, anxious, and tired, and eventually, you stop caring. You have a pit in your stomach, your heart races all day, and you are impatient. It starts as just a tiny feeling. Maybe you are slightly annoyed at first, but then the annoyance turns to anger. A few hours go by, and now you feel sad, anxious, and tired.*

It is not possible to entirely avoid negativity. It is all around us and comes from many different sources. Deal with it when it comes up so it does not build up.

Why It's Important

Negativity affects each person differently. It can affect how you feel and treat your customers, coworkers, friends, family, etc. It will rub off on your coworkers; you will feel it all day and probably take it home at the end of the day.

Negativity starts as a slight feeling and grows until you feel all these emotions simultaneously. It is overwhelming; if you do not deal with it, it will grow inside you and make things worse. Some days, it can be so bad that you want to clock out and leave.

Try your absolute best to avoid negativity and stop carrying it around. You feel so much better and enjoy your job more.

> **Hard Definition:**
>
> Do what you can every day to avoid negative thoughts, actions, and attitudes.
>
> Deal with any negativity when it comes up, and do not spread it.

How To "Avoid Negativity"

Stop yourself from thinking negative thoughts. Don't say it out loud. Don't think it. Don't mumble it under your breath. Don't say it to someone after the communication is over. Just don't. You need to break the habit of thinking and speaking negatively.

Implement steps to change your habits. This was a hard habit for me to break personally. You can do it; it will be worth it.

When a customer or peer says something negative, don't add your comment to it. Don't laugh or join in when others are negative. Either don't say anything or try to make it positive without arguing with your coworkers.

Use the "Don't Judge", "Be Polite", and "Listen to Understand" best practices to help you along the way. You will also learn other strategies to deal with negativity in the upcoming practices, "Bitch Session', "Recovery Time", and "Reset Button".

Surround yourself with positive things: pictures, sayings, photos, music, etc. Then, use those positive things to pull us out of the negativity.

Spread Positivity

Send coworkers positive messages when they are having a bad day. When others are being negative, make it a point to remain positive. Say something positive without rubbing it in others' faces or trying to make them feel bad for it. You do not have to call out your coworkers for being negative. You can focus on your work and tune out their negative conversations.

Do not commiserate with the customer or coworkers. Don't join in their negativity. You can express empathy without taking on their emotions, but it takes lots of practice. Stop yourself as soon as you realize you are doing it. You have to hold yourself accountable when you do and take action to break the habit.

You Are Not Responsible For The Customer's Emotions

You are not responsible for taking on customers' worries, emotions, or negative behavior as your own. You can still help customers solve their problems without accepting responsibility for all of their emotions. It is not your fault.

Let go of the customer's problems and emotions when the interaction ends. By that, I mean you can move on to your next customer or move on with your day as soon as you complete your tasks and the interaction with the customer is over. It is no longer your responsibility.

When a customer complains, whines, or puts people down, you don't have to agree with what they are saying or take on their emotions as your own. To avoid negativity, try showing understanding and empathy without agreeing with or commiserating with the customer. Listen to what they say and give a genuine statement of empathy that shows you understand and are going to help.

You have to decide that it is okay not to take responsibility for their problems. This doesn't mean you don't care about what they are going through and aren't going to help them solve the problem; it means your day doesn't have to be ruined because someone else is not behaving correctly.

Public Or Shared Spaces

The break room is a place for all employees to relax; if someone spreads negativity, you can ask them politely to stop. If they don't, you should leave and find another quiet place to let the negativity go. If you catch yourself being negative, apologize and try to create some positivity.

Release Any Built Up Negativity

Use any time available, like 1-on-1, team meetings, breaks, etc., to release the negativity. Talk with your coach or human resources department about the negativity. Find someone outside of work to talk to who can help release the negativity and provide some positivity.

Customers can be upset when something goes wrong. They may yell at you, insult you, or blame you personally, even though it is not your fault. Try to understand how important this might be to them and that we all tend to get emotional.

Showing some emotion is normal. A customer may overreact. While I do not enjoy rude customers, I try to understand their perspective and be forgiving. If it gets out of hand, escalate it to your supervisor.

Spreads Even When Working Remotely

Even though everyone is remote, it is still easy to spread negativity to coworkers. When someone is being negative, don't participate and try to create some positivity for yourself. If it worsens or impacts your ability to work, you should report it to your team leader or HR so they can handle it correctly.

Where Does The Negativity Go If You Don't Deal With It?

Unresolved negativity can go to many places, but in my experience, it comes out the most in your personal life. Ask yourself a few questions.

On your way home from work, have you ever:

- Scolded the cashier at the drive-thru window when you picked up dinner?
- Screamed or honked at every person you thought was driving like an "idiot" or cut you off?
- Overreacted to something small that went wrong?
- Fought with your kids, spouse, or partner as soon as you got home?

This is where the negativity goes when you don't deal with it. You take it out on everyone around you when you are angry, stressed, anxious, etc.. Eventually, it starts to impact your life. That is why it is essential to develop skills that help you avoid it rather than pick it up.

Be Ready When It Comes Up

Develop a strategy for dealing with it when it comes up. Make sure it actually works for you. It may take some time to find what works.

Put together a plan and try it for a while. Make changes when necessary. With practice, you can make this skill your strongest skill, and it will dramatically change your customer service career.

Notes:

Avoid Negativity

Reset Button

"I have to get rid of this feeling."

One day, while providing service, I reached a point where I hated how I felt, and I decided I would not let these mean, negative customers continue to destroy my feelings. I am usually quite happy and enjoy helping people, but that is not how I felt this day. I wanted to do something about it.

I went on my break to try to clear my mind so I would feel like me again. When I got back to my desk, I actually did feel better. I was happy again, and it felt great. Even my neighbors noticed that my mood had changed. When they asked me what I did, I told them I had just decided to reset myself and return to being my happy self.

Over the weekend, I realized how well it worked. I bought a big red novelty button with the word RESET printed on it. I put it on my desk for anyone to use. Now, if anyone needs to reset, they push the button and say, "Time to Reset".

This is going to last all day.

I noticed that if I had a bad call, it affected me for the rest of the day. It was a downward spiral; everything piled up, and some days, I did not make it until the end of the day and left early. After about a year, I realized I needed a way to deal with these calls better.

I came up with the idea of saying "Let it go" after difficult calls and trying to start the next call like a new day. It helps me release all that negativity. Sometimes, I will also take a deep breath, stand up, blow it out, and shake out my body. Sometimes, I do a little dance, anything that makes it go away.

What Is A "Reset Button"?

After every interaction, especially difficult ones, reset yourself so the next customer gets the same great experience as the last. Let go of what happened with the previous customer and start your next interaction free of judgment and ready to help.

Every customer deserves the same great experience; you can achieve that by resetting after every interaction. Clear your head of any emotion, frustration, or anxiety so you can continue with your day in a positive and healthier way.

When you have a difficult interaction, the negativity from that interaction can affect the next and every interaction after it. The next customer you interact with should not have to deal with the negativity from a previous customer, nor should you.

Why It's Important

No matter how long you have been in customer service, it affects you when customers are rude, offensive, and uncooperative. If you do not deal with the feelings created during these difficult interactions, they will continue to build up inside you and may cause serious problems.

If you reset after every interaction and use the "Don't Judge" and "Avoid Negativity" best practices, you can release those feelings and move on. You do not want to carry customer's negativity with you.

The next customer doesn't deserve mistreatment because the last person was cruel or unfair to you. Show each customer respect. You will be happier at the end of the workday, which will benefit your work and your personal life.

Your customer satisfaction ratings will increase, and you will be more satisfied with your job.

Hard Definition:

After each interaction, we must reset our attitude, emotions, and systems to start the next interaction without bias or judgment.

If we cannot reset on our own, we must ask someone for help.

How To Hit The "Reset Button"

After each interaction, do something to help you let go of what happened so you can treat the next customer with respect and provide the same excellent service you would have if the previous interaction had been positive.

Find something that works for you, something you can do after every interaction if necessary. Doing something physical creates a literal separation between each interaction. Don't just say it in your head.

Take a moment to calm down before your next interaction. Take a deep breath, and blow out the feelings. Blow them as far away as you possibly can. Stand up and walk around. Shake it out, literally. Shake your arms and legs, shoulders and head. Imagine the emotion of the last interaction falling off.

Whatever you decide to do, do it after every interaction to build a habit until it becomes natural. This habit will help you after even the most difficult interactions. If you do it consistently, you will start to reset automatically.

Actual Reset Button

If your workspace permits it, get a novelty red reset button, print a picture of a reset button, and place it on your desk, or hang it on the wall in your workspace. Place it at the end of your row so you can share it with your team. Make it a team goal to help each other overcome these challenging experiences.

Use It During An Interaction

It's hard to have someone yell at you, no matter who you are or how long you have been doing customer service. Whether you caused the problem or not, it is just uncomfortable. The best way to deal with this is to use all the best practices together and, when needed, use the "Reset Button."

Customers can express their emotions; they can yell, throw a tantrum, or swear, but no matter what, you are in control of your feelings.

Try to keep yourself calm and do not lose your temper. It can be challenging to do this when a customer is irrational and very upset. Use your "Be Polite", "Listen to Understand", and "Power of Oh" practices. These practices work well in these situations because they help you, too, not just the customer.

Listening instead of talking allows you to maintain control of your emotions and organize your thoughts before you respond. This is a form of resetting.

When needed, wait for a break in the conversation and ask if you can place them on hold for a moment or two. Make sure it is appropriate. Use this time to research their issue, calm down, gather, reset, and return to the conversation ready to help. Use your "Answer Confidently" and "Be A Guide "practices to provide a confident response and present a solution to the customer.

You Can Reset When In-Person

Unfortunately, if you are "in-person," resetting during an interaction is a little harder. Try to find something subtle and known only to you, such as folding a piece of paper in half a few times, crossing your fingers, or clasping your hands together and giving yourself a quick squeeze.

If you cannot reset during the interaction, be sure to take some time to reset afterwards.

Keep Your Personal Life Separate From Your Work Life

Keep your personal life and emotions out of your interactions with customers. If issues from your personal life keep popping up or bothering you, take some time away from production to deal with them.

If you are struggling personally, you will struggle to reset after difficult interactions. Find someone to talk to if you need help dealing with issues and work. It is a good idea to seek help dealing with life and work; it will help you deal with the day-to-day and let complex interactions go.

"I Am Not Mad At You..."

As customer service providers, we often hear, "I am not mad at you; I am mad at the company" or something else. The thing is, in many cases, it's true. We just have to believe it in order not to take it personally.

Let your customers vent. Be patient and hear them out. They need to feel heard, so let them vent.

Realize that what the customer is going through isn't your fault; we do not need to carry their emotional burden. You are probably thinking, "But wait, we have been told to empathize with our customers and try to understand what they are going through and meet them where they are and ...." Right. I am not saying stop doing those things; they are essential, but I am saying that you can do those things without carrying their emotional baggage.

Sneeze Guard

To help you deflect emotions, you need to put up a wall of sorts to keep them from getting all over you. Let me share an analogy with you.

Have you ever visited a sandwich shop or buffet-style restaurant with a clear plastic sneeze guard to protect the food? This is how I imagine my wall.

It is see-through so that I can see my customers, we can communicate, and I can still help them, but if they start "sneezing" their emotions all over me, I duck, and their emotions hit my sneeze guard instead of me.

From the customer's perspective, they were able to express their feelings; I heard them out and helped them solve their problem. From my perspective, I listened to the customer and helped them, but I didn't get any of their negative emotions on me. Now I can clean the glass, wipe off all the emotions, and go into my next call clean, reset, and ready to go.

Get Help From Your Coach Or Team Leader

Talk to your coach or team leader about your feelings and what is happening.

What did the customer do that made you so upset? Was that thing your fault, or did you cause it? No, probably not.

Should you allow this stranger to make you feel that way? No.

Are you just upset that they yelled at you, and you don't think that is right? Yes, and we agree. It's not right, but it happened, so you need to deal with it.

People Can Be Rude

Sometimes, people don't act or treat others the way they should. Try to remember that the customer is not mad at you. They are angry that something is wrong. Even if they treated you poorly, allow yourself to let go of it.

This is the exact reason "Reset Button" is a best practice. We want you to be okay at the end of every interaction and have no negativity. If you can't let it go, ask your coach or manager for help. You don't have to deal with it on your own.

Don't be offended. You cannot take what they did personally. Even when you helped and helped and helped, and they were unappreciative. Respond to their questions without bias. Take a deep breath, and let the emotion go.

Start the next interaction like it is a brand new one. Realize that the customer's problem is not your fault. Don't take on the blame. Focus on helping them find a solution.

Notes:

Reset Button

Use Recovery Time

"I have had enough!"

I have had days when I was very angry with customers. As I continued to take calls throughout the day, I started feeling impatient, and I wanted to be rude to them when they were rude to me. I had to keep pushing through to the end of the day. Then, one day, I was fed up. I felt like I could not do it anymore. After my call, I logged out and went outside.

While I was outside, I decided to walk around the building a couple of times. It calmed me down, and when I got back on the phone. I started to get customer compliments instead of complaints. I was surprised that I felt so much better.

"I don't know if I can keep going."

After a few difficult or confrontational interactions, it's hard to keep going. I would be rude or short with customers because I could not release those negative feelings. I would leave my phone in "after call work" to take some deep breaths and try to let it go, but some days, that is not enough.

On those days, I started getting off the phone, taking breaks early, or using some of my personal time. If the weather is good, I will go outside and walk around. If the weather is bad, I will go to another room where I could be alone. This would help release the tension and negativity, so the rest of my interactions with customers improved.

"Maybe you just need to take a few minutes."

I had a representative on my team who would leave early whenever they had a really bad interaction with a customer. They often talked to me about how they felt like quitting. I sympathized with them; customer service is hard. So, we devised a plan for them to take a few minutes off the phones to clear their head after they had a bad interaction.

Over time, I checked in on them, and their outlook improved a little bit every day; they were much happier than two weeks ago.

When I listened to their calls, they were performing better and happy to help customers again. I started doing this with all of my team members, and it had the same effect on everyone.

"Thank you for dealing with that."

I was reviewing a live call for one of my agents. It was a difficult interaction. The customer was upset and was not being fair with the agent. The agent handled the call reasonably well, but they were affected by it and needed a break.

I went to the agent's desk and said, "Thank you for dealing with the last call; it was tough. You are welcome to take some time off the floor to let it go." They were shocked to hear me say this and thanked me because that was tough for them.

When they returned, they stopped at my desk and thanked me again. I could tell they were feeling much better, and I was glad I could help. At our next team meeting, I told the rest of the team to ask if they needed time after a horrible interaction, and I would try to give it to them. They were so excited to have that option available to them.

After only a week, I started to notice a change in my team. They were no longer negative toward their job or customers and were not leaving work early because of horrible customers. I even had an agent tell me they were considering quitting, but they decided to stay and started to like their job again.

What Is "Use Recovery Time"?

Sometimes, interactions with customers do not go well. The customer may yell, constantly interrupt you, talk over the top of you, etc. This can leave you feeling really uncomfortable, argumentative, and defensive. Your heart is racing, your hands are shaking, and you feel overwhelmed. You must gather your thoughts and calm your emotions before you help the next customer.

Take some time after an interaction to let go of the negativity, frustration, fear, resentment, etc., that can build up while helping customers.

After a complicated interaction, you need to reset and release the negativity. Take the time when you need it, right after the interaction. Don't wait; the negativity will affect your interactions until you recover.

Why It's Important

Some interactions are more challenging than others, and providing good customer service and experiences is difficult all day. You need to release the negativity, reset yourself, and prepare for the next interaction so you feel better overall.

Taking time to recover will keep you positive, help maintain your job satisfaction, and help you provide great experiences for every customer.

> **Hard Definition:**
>
> After a difficult interaction with a customer, we must take time to recover before our next interaction.
>
> If we cannot recover on our own, we must ask someone for help.

How To "Use Recovery Time"

If you need to recover from a previous interaction, remove yourself from your production or work area and take the time to release the stress and negativity.

Get up from your desk for a few minutes to physically separate yourself from the interaction. This makes it easier for you to let go of it mentally.

Get a fresh glass of water, step outside to get some fresh air, and listen to a song you like that makes you feel happy.

Take that time to release any negativity and tension. Find a quiet room or go outside, breathe, and relax for a few minutes.

Do something physical like walking, dancing, shaking your arms and legs, jumping jacks, etc. Usually, it is best to do it yourself, but sometimes, a friend or coworker can help.

The trick is to find something that helps you deal with how it made you feel and get back to normal. You don't have to take a dance break if that doesn't work for you. It can be anything: do yoga or sing. Whatever works for you.

Don't be afraid to experiment with a few ideas to find what works.

Ask your coach or teammates for support if you need it.

My employer does not offer recovery time

You may need to use your break time or personal time. You may need to contact your HR to get some time approved. Work with your team leader and HR.

Notes:

Use Recovery Time

Improving Service

This section will teach you the best practices to improve your experiences.

Improving your experiences will require analysis and feedback from yourself, your coach, QA, coworkers, etc. Look for things you could improve on, then work to improve that area.

Feedback can be hard to hear and understand, but you need outside opinions to determine where and how to improve.

- Bitch Sessions
- Power-Up Sessions
- Continuous Improvement

Bitch Sessions

Gossiping about customers makes you feel worse.

One day, I was having a pretty hard time dealing with customers. It was one of those days when every customer called about the same thing, and they were all upset and argumentative. I was starting to get really frustrated explaining the same thing over and over. It got so bad that I started to complain to my coworkers about it, and then we started swapping bad customer stories.

After a few minutes, I realized I did not like how I sounded; I was whining. I felt terrible for being negative, and hearing them complain made me feel worse.

I asked my coach if I could talk to them about what had happened. As we talked, he said he understood and let me vent. After that, I felt so much better.

We started doing this every two weeks, and I stopped being so negative. I was handling challenging interactions much better. I had no more grudges and could focus on just helping the customers.

Sometimes, you just have to get it out.

I noticed agents were talking badly about our customers between calls. They were making fun of what they said and why they called in. They were being negative, and soon, our whole team became angry and hostile.

I pulled some agents that started it and took them to another room, where I asked what was bothering them. This allowed them to complain and get it out of their system. Meanwhile, the other agents on my team could focus on helping customers without hearing what these agents were complaining about.

When we were finished, the two agents I worked with calmed down and thanked me for letting them vent. They said it felt good to tell them what bothered them about customers and have someone listen.

This made me realize that sometimes it feels good to "bitch" about the things you don't like about your job. I started having regular meetings with several agents at a time to let them get it out.

I set up some ground rules. You are allowed to say whatever you want, as long as it was during the "Bitch Session" and away from production. During production, they were not allowed to complain or talk negatively about customers in production.

After about three weeks, we all noticed a big difference on the call floor. There was so much less negativity, and everyone was happier throughout the day overall.

What Are "Bitch Sessions"?

> *What is a bitch session? A discussion in which people complain or gripe, usually about a shared experience*
>
> *Dictionary.com*

For us, a "Bitch Session" is a specific time set aside to discuss your feelings about your customers and their actions. The purpose of an "Bitch Session" is to express negativity created by customers in a constructive way so it does not affect you, your customers, coworkers, and family.

Sometimes, negativity builds up, and we must get it out. We must let it go and stop carrying it with us all day.

A "Bitch Session" is also a safe place to express what you need to in order to eliminate negative feelings and prevent them from building up.

It is a safe place to vent your feelings and discuss your thoughts. It must be held outside of production when you are not interacting with customers and away from other providers, especially those interacting with customers. You don't want to spread negativity; you want to eliminate it.

Why It's Important

If that negativity is left to build, it will consume you and bring down your whole life, not just your work life. If the negativity is spread during production to your coworkers, they will return it and pile on top of you, leaving more for you to carry.

Customer service is a tough job, and carrying those negative feelings makes it harder to do your job; they make you feel awful inside and out and have a terrible impact on your personal life if you don't deal with them correctly.

Participating in "Bitch Sessions" allows you to learn about yourself and find new ways to handle difficult situations and negativity.

Dealing with the negativity is just as important as avoiding it. Carrying it around with you causes so many side effects it is not worth it.

> **Hard Definition:**
>
> We need to take time outside of production to complain or bitch to release any negativity or grudges we may have. This will prevent it from affecting us, our coworkers, and our interactions.
>
> This must be done every time you feel the negativity build up, like an itch you can't stop scratching.

How To Use "Bitch Sessions"

Take some time away from production to talk about what is bothering you. You can talk about how annoying customers are or how you hate having to waive late fees. Get it out and let it go. Don't spread it to your coworkers or customers.

We have found that talking about it this way will help you deal with your feelings constructively; when you are done, you won't feel like yelling at the customer, telling them off, or calling them names.

Whenever you have a bad or negative experience with a customer and can't seem to get rid of the negativity, ask your leader for time to have an "Bitch Session."

I keep notes about what bothers me during the gaps between sessions. This way, when I get the chance, I don't forget something and get it off my chest.

"Bitch Sessions" should be held away from everyday workspaces and offices. Find a different room or office away from work and break areas. It should also be a place where others cannot eavesdrop on what is being said.

How To Bitch Effectively

Get the negativity out in a constructive way. Don't just complain or call the customer names. Discuss what bothered you and try to understand why. Then, talk about how to handle it differently next time.

During a "Bitch Session," it is okay to admit that you feel the customer was stupid, arrogant, mean, or annoying. We should not call the customer stupid, irritating, idiot, or moron. Do not use curse words or negative phrases or make inappropriate comments. Name-calling will not help you deal with the negativity; it will make you feel worse.

Talk about your thoughts and feelings, but be careful of how you talk about them—instead of saying, "They were so stupid, I could not believe it", say what the customer did that made you feel that way. For example, "I kept saying, 'Please click on Settings,' and then they would click on something different. I explained where the button was, but they could not see it. It pissed me off because it is right there, it's blue, it's in the top right corner, you can't miss it. It made me feel like they were stupid." Saying it this way is much more productive to discuss the scenario than name-calling. This will help you better understand what happened and how it made you feel.

Take a self-analysis to ensure nothing personal is getting in the way, and look for a better way to deal with your feelings.

- Were you judging the customer for something they said or did not know how to do?
- Are you being short and impatient because you are having a bad day?
- Are you annoyed with the customer just for calling or coming into the store?

Learning to understand and deal with it means walking through the interaction from the beginning, breaking down what happened, and discussing it. As you go through it, you will feel the same emotions it made you feel when it happened. Take a few deep breaths and talk about how it made you feel when the customer said that to you.

- What did you want to say back to them?
- Why do you think the customer behaved the way they did?

Try to understand why you feel the customer behaved the way they did. This is not to justify their actions but to help you process how they made you feel and affect you. This will help you understand that it wasn't your fault and that you did not deserve to be treated that way. Understanding this makes it easier to release these emotions and move on positively.

How To Do It On Your Own

If your leader does not provide time, you can still have an "Bitch Session" on your own. Write down your feelings on a piece of paper or notes app. Write down why you are feeling that way. Try to think of any way to handle it differently and who you could ask for advice. Write these down, too.

Read through it a couple of times, and then when your BiItch Session" is over, let the negativity go. Don't keep it around; this will help you let it go.

Notes:

Power-Up Sessions

I want my team to be the best

I wanted my team to be the best in the company. When I noticed something specific that a provider was struggling with, I would schedule 15-30 minutes with them, and we would focus on helping improve on that one subject. We had few distractions and could practice more than during other meetings. My agents liked the focused time, and it was very effective.

I hate explaining residual interest; they never seem to understand it

I hated explaining residual interest. No matter how I did it, the customer never seemed to understand it. I asked my coach if I could use my weekly training time to listen to calls where other agents explained it to their customers so I could learn to do it better.

During the first 20 minutes, I listened to the calls of five other agents and spent the rest of the time practicing and perfecting my explanation.

After hearing other agents do it, I felt more confident and stopped shying away from explaining it to customers. I even started teaching other agents my new way of doing it.

What Are "Power-Up Sessions"?

Choose a specific area where you need to improve, then focus on that area to improve. This is how you can level up your skills. The name "Power-Up" comes from video games. When you find a specific item, usually hidden, you gain more power or health in the game, aka "Power-Up". You continue to be from a better position because you have more "life" or "health" in the game.

These sessions are meant to be short but effective. Talk through the most challenging situations at your job and find ways to make them more accessible.

Work with your teammates and coach. Ask for advice, review other interactions, and practice until you reach your desired skill level.

Why It's Important

Each session will improve your skills and make our job easier. It will help you feel more comfortable and capable and will create more confidence in your ability to do your job. This could lead to a raise or a promotion.

You will learn new and better ways to do things. Working with others allows you to learn from their techniques and approaches. You will see how other providers handle the same situation, and then you can apply that knowledge to your interactions.

It will expand your current skillset. Every "Power-Up Session" can help you get a new skill or improve your current skill. If you are applying for a promotion, work on the skills most important to the new position.

> **Hard Definition:**
>
> We must spend dedicated time focused on improving in a specific area or topic.

How to Use "Power-Up Sessions"

Select a specific subject or something you need or want to improve on. It can be a particular scenario, policy, or procedure. Is there anything you want to improve upon? It can also be a new skill or improving your statistics or bonuses—anything to help you improve and gain more confidence or experience.

Session Ideas

- Angry customer calling about a complicated issue
- Customer returning a defective item
- Complex or new company policy
- Failed QA review
- Practice greetings and rebuttals
- Create new upsell strategies or scripts
- Review recent difficult interactions
- Improve your "Don't Judge" skills
- Learn how to say things in a more polite tone
- Practice your technique to "Avoid Negativity"
- Focus on your communication skills for emails or texts
- Practice "Answer Confidently"

- Review the process and "How To" documents for the task(s) you struggle with most

Make A Plan

Once you have decided on the subject matter, set at least one goal to achieve during the session or sessions. If you are trying to improve your statistics, set a target like increasing customer satisfaction rating by 10% or decreasing average handle time by 15 seconds. If you are trying to improve your confidence or experience, give yourself a current rating of a number between 1 and 10. After the session, rate yourself again to see if you feel an improvement.

Find interactions you can review. They can be your own and from other providers; use the best you can find.

Work with your coach or team leader. They can provide examples, resources, experts, and more. They can also help you set your goals and determine whether you have achieved them.

Gather information and past interactions involving the subject matter and then learn from them. Fix mistakes and practice different approaches and techniques. Focus on getting better.

Keep Track Of Your Interactions

Write down the date and time of interactions that pertain to the subject matter. Have your coach, QA, or team members review the interactions and give you feedback. It may be hard to hear their opinions, but this feedback will help you grow and reach your goals.

Find an expert to work with; if a coworker is better or has more experience, work with them to get advice and learn from their example. Have them review your interactions and give you feedback. Ask them questions and practice a few scenarios with them. Try to understand their techniques and phrasing and apply them to your interactions.

Longer Term Goals

Some goals may take more than one session to achieve; select a skill or subject you want to focus on every two weeks. During the next two weeks, try to plan training, practice, co-working, etc., to help you improve on the selected subject.

Once you have chosen a topic, please share it with your coach. They should be able to provide material, sample interactions to observe, and activities that will help you improve.

Work on this subject as much as possible. Conduct as many "Power-up Sessions" as you need to meet your goals.

Someone In Another Department or Job

Once per month, try to work with another employee from another department or position. Work with them for a few hours to learn more about their department and the processes they perform.

Try to get some time away from production, at least 15 minutes, where you can focus on a complicated subject. Ask your coach or team leader to find interactions from other providers that you can listen to or read.

More Advanced Session Ideas

Don't Judge Session

If you judged a customer, ask yourself why. This will require a lot of self-exploration and honesty. If you are not honest with yourself about why you judged them, you will not be able to move past it or overcome it.

Avoid Negativity Session

When you feel negative and jaded and no longer enjoy your job, ask yourself why. Again, be honest. Find a technique that works for you. It should help you return to your normal state of being, free of the emotions created by the customer. This is a hard skill to master and takes lots of practice.

Difficult Customers Session

Make a plan for how you will handle the most difficult customers or other situations you struggle with. Define what you will do ahead of time so that when a customer interrupts you, argues, or is rude, you already know what to do. For example, I had a really hard time not arguing back with my customers.

I decided to learn to manage all of the emotions that came up with confrontational customers and stop arguing with them.

When a customer interrupts me, I will stop talking as soon as I realize it and let them speak first.

When the customer becomes argumentative, I count to two in my head before I respond to slow the pace of the conversation and give myself time to think before I respond.

I decided to listen to understand their perspective and always follow it up with an apology or show of empathy.

I decided to always use a polite and professional tone of voice and never treat a customer with disrespect, even when they were cruel and made me cry.

Notes:

Continuous Improvement

How do I get promoted

I wanted a promotion because I wanted more money. I worked for this company for 15 months but was not promoted. I asked my team leader, "How do I get promoted?" They scheduled some time for us to meet and go over my stats. Most of my stats were above average but stayed the same for about five months.

He said when I apply for a promotion, they will look at the stats and want to see that they are improving over time. We made a plan for me to work on each statistic over the next two months, and I would focus on a specific statistic for two weeks at a time.

At the end of the two months, I had improved; I applied for the promotion and got it. My team leader told me I could have gotten it earlier if my stats had shown improvement.

"How are you always one of the top agents?"

I have worked as a customer service agent at the same company for seven years. I have been a senior agent, co-advisor, and team leader. Whenever I get new agents on my team, they always ask me how I was able to be one of the top agents so consistently.

I always share a few tips with them and advise that listening to other agents is a great way to diversify your skills. Every two weeks, I would ask to pair up with another top agent and listen to a few of their calls. I would take notes, write down what they did differently, and then apply those to my calls. Doing this regularly allowed me to listen to over 40 agents, and I always found new ways to do it better.

I hate the awkward feeling of not knowing what to do

I want to be as prepared as possible when answering phone calls or working with customers in person. I hate the awkward feeling of not knowing what to do. Whenever I ran into a rare situation with a customer, I would try to do my best, and then, after the interaction was complete, I would try to find other examples to learn from.

I would ask the other agents and coaches if they had ever dealt with that situation and how they handled it. Then, I would practice dealing with this situation, and when it came up again, I was prepared and did not feel awkward. I was confident that I could help the customers.

What Is "Continuous Improvement"?

We should always strive to improve and keep our skills fresh by learning new and better ways to do things. We should work with peers to learn as much as possible from each other. This must happen continuously, once every week, but at least once a month.

Make a plan and schedule time to improve your skills and confidence. Keep this plan current and plan your work for the next three months.

Why It's Important

Providing good service takes continuous practice to keep our skills sharp. It can be easy for our improvement to plateau or slow down, but implementing an ongoing process can prevent that.

If you aim to get a promotion or higher bonus, this will help keep you on track.

Even after 22 years of providing customer service, I still have days where I let negativity get to me or judge customers. I always go back, look at what I did, and learn from my mistakes. Re-evaluating how I handled it allows me to know more about myself so that I can do better.

> **Hard Definition:**
>
> We must analyze our interactions regularly and set goals we want to achieve. For each goal, create actionable recommendations and a plan to implement them.

How To Implement "Continuous Improvement"

Find Ways To Improve

Look for ways that you can learn something new. Ask to attend training classes, participate in role plays, and practice scenarios with new agents. Have a "Power-Up Session" with a coach, QA, etc. Find tutorials and practice on our own time. Participate in "Itch Sessions".

Review Your Work

Every month, review some of your interactions and grade yourself. When you find an area where you need to improve, dedicate some months to work on it. Compare your scores to the previous months to ensure you are improving.

Ask others to evaluate you. Although outside opinions can be hard to hear sometimes, they are a great way to learn things about ourselves that we could not see on our own.

After each QA review, take time to learn from the review.

Make a Plan

Use "Power-Up" sessions to focus on improving specific areas. You should have one at least every two weeks, make a plan to improve, and work towards your goals.

Once a month, ask your team leader about areas where you can improve. If you are interested in a promotion, ask about the skills you will need to fulfill that position and make a plan to improve in each area. Plan to work on at least one of their suggestions during the month.

Set Goals

Be sure the goals you set are specific and achievable. It should be a small step up from where you are now. It does not have to be a huge jump. For example, you should set a goal to increase your CSAT score from 75% to above 85%. This goal is very achievable and also realistic. Expecting to jump from 75% to 100% within a few days or weeks is extremely difficult and probably impossible.

Don't shoot yourself in the foot by setting a goal you can never achieve. This puts a lot of unnecessary pressure on you daily, which can be very stressful.

Focus On One Problem At A Time

If you have missed a step multiple times, focus on fixing that problem. Make sure you do it on every call, chat, and email. Set a goal to get it right on all QAs that month. This goal is very achievable. Also, focusing your energy on remembering that step will build muscle memory so that it becomes a habit, and you may never miss it again.

Create Actionable Recommendations

For each area you want to improve, create actionable recommendations for yourself. Simply put, define specific actions that will help you improve. Do not recommend something you will never be able to accomplish.

For example, if you want to increase your customer satisfaction rating (CSAT), you could recommend being nicer to customers, but this will go nowhere because it is not specific. A better recommendation would be always to say thank you when a customer answers your question.

Break big recommendations into smaller, easier-to-implement ones. You should make these changes incrementally. Work on smaller improvements until you have achieved your bigger goal.

For each recommendation, make a plan for implementing it. The plan can be very simple. For example, Create a sticky note that says "Ask Question? Say Thank You!" and put it on your screen. Having a plan will help during the provide phase when you get busy. You can read the plan over again and start working on it.

Notes:

Continuous Improvement

Summary

These best practices are meant to be applied together, layered one on top of the other, as needed, during any interaction. Together, they are even more effective and will ensure you always provide the best experiences possible.

It's hard to define a great experience, and it can differ for each customer and situation. If you use best practices, are willing to help, and do everything you can for the customer, you can be confident that you provided the best experience possible.

Customers don't always get what they want, but you can still provide a great experience. Discounts or free items do not guarantee a great experience; they are most likely unnecessary.

You will have to learn as you go, but you will start to find your way. Leverage all the resources in this book and our website, https://bestcxever.com/provider, to guide you as you interact with your customers.

The more you practice, the better you will get. Family and friends can make great fake customers and enjoy acting out different scenarios.

Providing Great Experiences to Bad Customers

You can't always give the customer what they want, but this does not determine if it was a great experience. Some customers try to make it seem like that and will give you a bad review. These are not fair because the customer is behaving incorrectly. They are rude and threatening to scare you into giving them what they want. This is the most challenging part of being a customer service provider.

It may not feel like it, but you can still provide these customers with a great experience. If you remained calm, professional, and polite while they were rude, if you waited for them to finish speaking, even when they interrupted you, if you guided them to a solution and provided all of the possible options, then you provided the customer with a great experience and can be proud of your hard work.

If you learn and apply what you learn in this book, you can provide your customers with great experiences, even the bad ones.

Company Policy Created the Bad Experience

Providing an extraordinary experience is in your control, no matter what company policies you have to follow.

As customer service providers, we may not always agree with company policy and may get upset that we cannot make an exception for the customer in this situation. Understanding that you can still provide a good experience in these situations is essential.

You can still be polite, communicate clearly, and guide the customer toward a solution, even if you disagree with the policies. Our job is to provide a great experience and uphold the rules simultaneously.

Use these best practices to help you balance following the rules and providing great experiences.

You Are Ready To Help

If you follow this book's advice and best practices, you will be ready to help any customer anytime. You are prepared to help any customer at any company, even without training. You can walk into any company and start supporting its customers on the spot.

How We Can Help You

We offer training classes to help you learn and implement our best practices. In our training classes, we dive deeper into the practices and share more examples from other great providers. During the class, you will work directly with one of our trainers, an expert on our best practices. They will create personalized examples and tips for you and your industry or company.

We also offer consulting, where you will work one-on-one with our experts. They will provide personalized advice, help with challenging scenarios, create custom scripts and rebuttals, and help you deal with the negativity and stresses of delivering great customer experiences. They can even provide tips and advice to help you get raises, promotions, or high bonuses.

If you own a business, work a side hustle, or are interested in starting one, we have a book, training classes, and consulting for our best practices for owners.

We have resources to help you remember and implement the best practices you just learned. We have posters, flip cards, reset buttons, etc. You can view the available products and services at https://bestcxever.com/provider.

Appendix

The Customer Experience

Here is a list of available jobs that focus entirely on the customer's experience. These jobs were all available when this book was printed.

Customer Experience Strategist DEPARTMENT OF THE TREASURY Internal Revenue Service

---

CUSTOMER EXPERIENCE Mobile Expert, Virtual Retail Apply Now

CUSTOMER EXPERIENCE Customer Service Account Associate Apply Now

---

BUSINESS OPERATIONS Sr Resolution Excellence Manager Apply Now

---

Radiology Scheduler SquarePeg United States

Customer Success Associate - Fully Remote CINQ PARTNERSHIP United States Apply

---

Customer Experience Rep. CropX United States Apply

Customer Care Manager - REMOTE MasteryPrep Dallas, TX Apply

Customer Experience Quality Assessor - Remote PharmaCentra, LLC - Administrative Americus, GA Apply

---

Customer Experience Specialist Ascen United States Apply

Customer Success Specialist (Ora) Ora Dental United States Apply

Appendix

Client Success Associate (Entry level, Remote) INFUSE Chicago, IL Apply

---

Customer Experience Specialist Flock Safety Atlanta, GA Apply

---

Customer Success Consultant - Remote Frontline Performance Group Winter Park, FL Apply

---

Customer Experience Manager SoloSuit United States Apply

Vice President of Customer Experience Peek United States Apply

---

Customer Success Manager (Remote US, EST) Fortanix New York, NY Apply

---

Customer Support Specialist Rinsed United States Apply

Customer Experience (CX) Intern Actian Corporation Remote, OR Apply

---

Principal Specialist, User Experience (UX)/ Customer Experience (CX) Aptive Remote, OR Full-Time Apply

---

Customer Experience (CX) Specialist Peraton Atlanta, GA Full-Time Apply

---

Customer Experience (CX) Designer Navistar, Inc. Lisle, IL Full-Time Apply

---

Sr Project Manager with CX (Customer Experience) Keylent Remote, OR Full-Time Apply

---

CX Business Analyst - REMOTE PTP Sacramento, CA Full-Time Apply

---

Customer Experience / Partnership Specialist - Parentfile - Remote Your SmartSource Petaluma, CA $70,000 to $80,000 Yearly Full-Time Apply

Appendix

Principal CX/UX Research Consultant - Remote R0041305 Wolters Kluwer DXG U.S., Inc. Remote, OR Full-Time Apply

Customer Experience Analyst Lead Oculus Sunnyvale, CA $110,000 Yearly Full-Time Apply

Training and Quality Specialist, CX Tools for Humanity San Francisco, CA $100,000 Yearly Apply

CX Consultant Zoom Video Communications, Inc. Seattle, WA $186,200 Yearly Full-Time Apply

Client Support Specialist BodySpec Phoenix, AZ Full-Time Apply

CX CONTACT CENTER MANAGER Shell Energy Solutions Houston, TX Full-Time Apply

Regional Marketing / CX Manager Waste Connections Fife, WA Full-Time Apply

Customer Experience Manager (Enterprise Accounts) - US Roambee Santa Clara, CA Full-Time Customer Experience Manager (Enterprise Accounts) – US (any location) Apply

Sr. Customer Experience Account Specialist - Remote JOB REF: 162016 LOCATION: Chesterfield, NH 03443 CATEGORY: Customer Experience JOB TYPE: Full-time

Answer Confidently

Here are the answers to the practice questions we provided:

- How tall is the Empire State Building/Eiffel Tower?
    - 1,250 feet (380 meters) / 984 feet (300 meters)
- How tall is the Eiffel Tower?
    - 984 feet (300 meters)
- What is the population of the USA in 2022?
    - 333.3 million
- What is the square root of 2478?
    - 49.7795
- How much does the International Space Station weigh?
    - 925,000 pounds (420,000 kilograms)
- What is the speed of light?
    - 299,792,458 meters per second / 186000 miles/sec
- How big is the Indian Ocean?
    - 27.24 million sq miles
- What is the longest road in the US?
    - US Route 2 at 3,365 miles
- How many permanent seats does the Indianapolis Motor Speedway in Indiana, USA have?
    - 235,000
- What is the melting point of Magnesium?
    - 1,202°F or 650°C
- How many seconds are in 6 days?
    - 518400

Bibliography

pg 11: "experience ." The Oxford Pocket Dictionary of Current English, 11 June 2018, https://www.encyclopedia.com/philosophy-and-religion/philosophy/philosophy-terms-and-concepts/experience.

pg 11: "experience ." Cambridge Dictionary, (n.d.), https://dictionary.cambridge.org/us/dictionary/english/experience.

pg 11: "service ." Cambridge Dictionary, (n.d.), https://dictionary.cambridge.org/us/dictionary/english/service.

pg 11: "service ." Merriam-Webster, (n.d.), https://www.merriam-webster.com/dictionary/service.

pg 17: Maxwell, John C. (2012). The 15 Invaluable Laws of Growth: Live Them and Reach Your Potential. Center Street.

pg 18: Confucius. Tamblyn, Nicholas. (2016). The Complete Confucius: The Analects, The Doctrine Of The Mean, and The Great Learning.

pg 19: Elevate Society. (2024). All good thoughts and ideas mean nothing without action. https://elevatesociety.com/all-good-thoughts-and-ideas.

pg 19: BoonePickens.com. (n.d.). Telling it Like it is. https://boonepickens.com/?page_id=1283.

pg 19: Maxwell, John C. (2003). "Thinking for a Change: 11 Ways Highly Successful People Approach Life and Work". Hachette.

pg 23: "best practice ." Merriam-Webster, (n.d.), https://www.merriam-webster.com/dictionary/best%20practice.

pg 42: "issue ." Merriam-Webster, (n.d.), https://www.merriam-webster.com/dictionary/issue.

pg 48: "feedback ." Oxford Learner's Dictionary, (n.d.), https://www.oxfordlearnersdictionaries.com/us/definition/english/feedback.

pg 48: "feedback ." Britannica Dictionary, (n.d.), https://www.britannica.com/dictionary/feedback.

Bibliography

pg 54: Kaye, Sarah. No Matter the Wreckage: Poems, (n.d.), https://www.amazon.com/No-Matter-Wreckage-Sarah-Kay/dp/1938912489.

pg 170: "bitch session ." Dictionary.com, (n.d), https://www.dictionary.com/browse/bitch-session.

Author Bios

Kirstla Ostler

I have worked in customer service for 25 years. I have worked for many major companies in the shipping, fast food, market research, financial, real estate, and healthcare industries. I worked my way up to being an advisor, guru, quality assurance, trainer, team leader, and manager.

I have also worked as a quality assurance manager and phone center manager. I have worked with owners to help them improve their customer service processes and train their providers to be the best.

I am a business owner and a lifelong customer service. I love interacting with customers and use these best practices every day.

I am excited to teach you our best practices and look forward to working with you.

Shawn Ostler

I have over 25 years of experience in the customer service industry. I am proud to say that I have worked with many high-profile companies in the financial, hospitality, real estate, health care, and retail sectors, helping them develop customer experiences, writing scripts and practice scenarios, and more.

I have worked with small and large business owners, teaching them how to implement the practices that will result in the best customer experiences. I have also consulted on their business plans, marketing strategies, and product lines.

I have also worked in sales as a salesperson and sales manager. I have written training materials and scripts that dramatically increased sales and customer service ratings.

I look forward to teaching you our best practices and assisting you with anything else you need.

www.ingramcontent.com/pod-product-compliance
Lightning Source LLC
Chambersburg PA
CBHW052150220526
45471CB00004B/1609